Cohen's

A Northamptonshire
railway graveyard

Jeffery Grayer

© Jeffery Grayer 2018

ISBN 978 0 86093 680 0

First published 2018 by Crécy Publishing Ltd

A CIP record for this book is available from the British Library

Publisher's Note: Every effort has been made to identify and correctly attribute photographic credits. Any error that may have occurred is entirely unintentional.

Printed in Turkey by Olas Solutions

Crécy Publishing Limited
1a Ringway Trading Estate
Shadowmoss Road
Manchester M22 5LH

www.crecy.co.uk

Front cover A graphic illustration of the brutal nature of the destruction involved in scrapping a steam locomotive is provided by this view of Midland 4F No. 44278 captured at Cohen's Cransley yard on 30 May 1966. An essential ingredient of the scrapman's arsenal, the red oxy acetylene gas bottle, takes centre stage whilst assorted debris lies scattered around the site. The unusual rural nature of the scrapyard here is apparent in the verdant backdrop to the scene. *Derek Fear*

Frontispiece This April 1969 view reveals that a Stanier '8F' has already lost its smokebox door and part of the smokebox cladding whilst in the foreground sets of wheels plus a chimney bear mute testimony to the demise of former Midland compatriots. *George Woods*

Rear cover, main image A scrapyard view dating from 10 May 1978 with Class 25 No. 25056 on the thrice weekly freight service which took away loaded scrap from Cransley. *Lewis Bevan*

Rear cover, inset top Adding much needed colour to the sombre shades of the scrapyard were a number of LT Underground cars which were captured at Cransley on 4 April 1964. *Ron Fisher*

Rear cover, inset middle Separated from their tenders and with boiler lagging draped over the running plates the locomotives in front of 'Black 5' No. 44906 make for a sombre scene on 4 August 1968. *Derek Fear*

Rear cover, inset lower Retaining its original green livery, 'Derby Lightweight' motor coach E79025 awaits its fate on 21 June 1970. *Gordon Edgar*

Map on p4 Map reproduced by kind permission of the of the Ordnance Survey

Contents

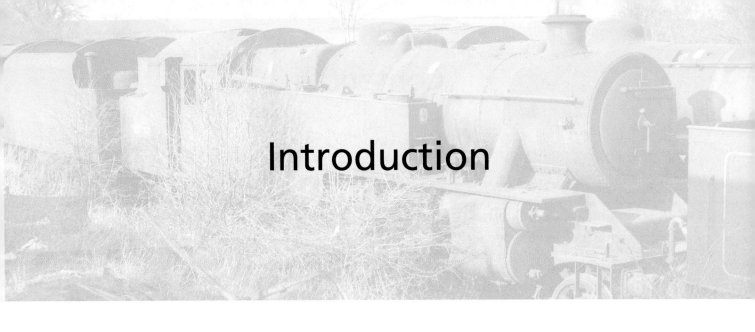

Introduction

If I should die, think only this of me:
That there's some corner of a foreign field
That is for ever England. There shall be
In that rich earth a richer dust concealed;
A dust whom England bore . . .

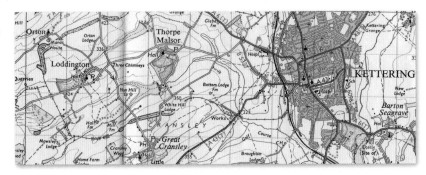

These famous lines from Rupert Brooke's 1914 poem *The Soldier* could perhaps be applied to the death of a railway locomotive, so many of which met their end many miles from their home regions in a bucolic setting in rural Northamptonshire. Images of withdrawn railway stock evoke sad memories of happier times and provide a stark contrast to their operational days and this is particularly so when they are being dismembered with the aid of oxy-acetylene torches, hammers and crowbars by the employees of a scrapyard. Such destruction is rendered more poignant when, as in this case, it took place against a background not of a grimy industrial landscape but with green fields and verdant woods as a backdrop. This volume follows on from my earlier book *Visions of Barry* which dealt with the famous scrapyard of Woodham & Sons in South Wales and covers another of the major firms involved in the mammoth task of cutting up BR's unwanted fleet.

The firm of George Cohen Sons & Co. has a long history going back to its foundation in 1834 but in the 1960s and beyond they became well known to the railway fraternity in their role as one of more than 100 contractors involved in the scrapping of the BR fleet of steam and diesel locomotives. As we shall see they also handled diesel multiple units, industrial steam and diesel locomotives and even the odd electric locomotive and bizarrely some ancient London Transport Tube stock at their Cransley site plus the more 'bread and butter' work of reducing coaches and wagons to scrap.

I am grateful to the many contributors to this volume as, never having been lucky enough to visit the site near Kettering in its heyday, I have had to tell the story without the benefit of first-hand knowledge. These are acknowledged at the end of this volume as are the various sources used in the compilation of the data. Today the site of the former scrapyard is being covered with industrial units the occupants of which will in all likelihood be completely unaware of the activity that went on there more than 50 years ago.

Jeffery Grayer
Devon, 2018

1

BR Scrapping Policy & External Contractors

The various Works of the British Railways (BR) regions had traditionally handled the scrapping of withdrawn locomotives since the earliest days of railways and in the period from 1955 to the mid 1960s there were some 19 such locations throughout the country involved in this task. The Southern Region (SR) of BR continued to undertake the task of ridding itself of unwanted steam locomotives at its own workshops right up to early 1964 when it became apparent that the capacity of its in-house scrapping facilities

was becoming increasingly inadequate with log jams of condemned locomotives cluttering up yards and sidings throughout the region. This led the SR to follow the lead of other BR regions and outsource the scrapping operation to a number of outside contractors who bid for withdrawn stock in the usual closed tender process. Much of the scrapping was done in South Wales, home of the major players such as Cashmore's and Buttigieg's of Newport, Woodham's of Barry together with Bird's of Morriston,

Standard tank No. 80132 being cut up by Cohen's "Flying Cutters" outside the front of the steam shed at Eastleigh on 19th. March 1966. Visible in the left background is M7 No. 30053 stored pending its removal to the USA. The Drummond tank was of course subsequently repatriated. *George Woods*

Following the end of steam on the SR in July 1967 Standard 2-6-0 No. 76008 is seen at the rear of Weymouth shed on the 8th. July prior to removal to Cohen's Cransley for scrapping. Built at Horwich in February 1953 it was withdrawn in April 1967. Note the motion tied up with rope whilst the missing connecting rods are undoubtedly stowed in the tender. *Derek Jones*

Risca, Bynea and Bridgend and Ward's of Briton Ferry. The other regions of BR had been using outside contractors for some time, amongst whose ranks was the firm of George Cohen who had a number of yards, that at Cransley near Kettering being the subject of this volume.

As long ago as March 1959 the Western Region had begun using external contractors in the shape of Woodham Brothers when four locomotives were despatched from Swindon to Barry in South Wales. This first movement in what was to become a vast exodus of steam from BR ownership really had its origins the previous year when a re-appraisal of the 1955 Modernisation Plan led to the acceleration of the disposal rate of the steam fleet such that the expectation was that they would all be gone within 10 years. This followed from the downturn in freight traffic and the rise in wages and materials costs in the overoptimistic hope that getting rid of steam would return the railways to profit within five years. This was to prove a forlorn hope as we now know. By the early 1960s some 100 firms, ranging in size from what might be described as Grade 1 yards as mentioned above who handled hundreds of locomotives to small outfits cutting just a handful, were involved in this mammoth scrapping process. The yards of George Cohen could be classed as belonging to the second tier of such scrap merchants cutting, as they did, appreciable quantities of stock.

Employees of Cohen's also travelled to various locations, including several on the SR, to cut up locomotives that were unfit to travel, these included 'Merchant Navy' 35004

Cunard White Star, Maunsell Moguls 31619/31809/31866, 'Q1' 33015, Standard Class 5 73041, Standard tank 80132 and 'USA' tanks 30066/30074 in their departmental guise as DS235/236 all at Eastleigh and 'N' Mogul 31850 at Redhill shed. Cohen's 'Flying Cutters', as they were known, also attended to a couple of Standard tanks, 80096 and 80102, on a site at Ringwood in Hampshire. They were often relatively small teams of dismantlers, for example just three men attended to 31809/31866 and 80132 at Eastleigh in the spring of 1966. They also visited sites on other regions such as Bletchley and Stratford sheds where in each location a solitary diesel shunter was scrapped. Cohen's were not the only firm whose employees travelled to sheds on the SR to undertake cutting. Standard Class 5 73170 and Class 4 76053 were both cut up at Weymouth shed by Cashmore's of Newport. After the end of steam traction on the SR in July 1967 Cohen's connection with the SR was to continue into the post steam age as electric locomotive No. 74006, formerly E5023, which had been withdrawn from Eastleigh in June 1976 due to fire damage, was noted in the yard at Cransley in 1977. This was the only Class 74 to be broken up here. Previously Bulleid-Raworth electric locomotive No. 20003 had arrived in the yard in 1969 from Durnsford Road, Wimbledon. The locomotive, which had been withdrawn in November 1968, spent some time at Brighton Top Goods Yard before being towed to Durnsford Road on 15 December where it was used as a generator by the CM&EE's (Chief Mechanical & Electrical Engineers) department until

1969. It was noted in sidings near Kettering the following October, being scrapped by Cohen's a month afterwards.

The other regions of BR, notably the Western (WR) and the Midland (MR), also made good use of Cohen's Cransley facility with the WR sending 26, and the MR no less than 164 locomotives to the Northamptonshire site for disposal. In the diesel age over 130 locomotives met their end here and diesel and electric multiple units were also to be seen at Cransley. Many coaches and freight vehicles were also broken up here together with industrial steam and diesel locomotives. Transactions were by competitive tender, the highest bid securing the sale, but the scrap merchant usually had to factor in the cost of movement by rail from the BR site to his yard and this could add as much as £200 to the price although in some cases there was an option indicating 'Carriage paid by BR'. As transactions increased in number the locomotives were no longer sent from BR Works but from their home shed which broadened the scope considerably and reduced the cost of transit and encouraged more local yards to bid for locomotives made redundant in their home area. As numbers of yards increased and scrapyards became more proficient at handling throughput, it made long distance movements more worthwhile but even so there were some surprisingly long journeys made by SR locomotives to Rotherham, Norwich and Swansea.

In 1964/5 it was a condition of sale that the copper firebox of a loco sold for scrap to a private yard should be returned to BR. Most went to Derby where stripped of all foreign metal they were melted down and re-forged as copper wire for West Coast Main Line (WCML) electrification. Oddly BR did not always reclaim the fireboxes they were entitled to and lines of neatly stacked fireboxes could be seen at scrapyards awaiting collection that never came. Some of the sales correspondence reveals complaints from scrap dealers that often quite significant items were missing from locomotives upon receipt for example coupling rods, boiler mountings and injectors. Instructions duly went out that each locomotive should be inspected before departure and that under no circumstances should parts be removed for use as spares for other locomotives without prior authority. Items which could be legitimately removed before sale were the smokebox door numberplate, the depot allocation plate and the works plates. Of course tenders should have been emptied of coal and boilers emptied of water but again this did not always happen. Where parts were missing they were often located and subsequently sent on eg four connecting rods, eight coupling rods and 15 elements from Standards 82015 and 73074 were despatched in a wagon to Cashmore's of Newport in February 1965. Portable equipment such as lamps, shovels, fire irons and potentially hazardous items such as the engine's stock of detonators were removed. Connecting rods were often taken off and sometimes thrust unceremoniously into firebox doors. Valve gear linkages were partly dismantled and tied up with rope. Movement of dead engines was governed by 'Special Notices' which specified the exact running of the train, where and when stops were to be made for examination, primarily for 'hot box' detection,

U Class No.31619 reduced to its frames at Eastleigh Works in March 1966 by Cohen's men as, by this time, in-house scrapping at the works had come to an end. Another Maunsell Mogul awaits similar treatment behind. *Peter Yarlett*

Standard Class 4 Mogul 2-6-0 No. 76053 captured in the freight yard at Weymouth is seen in the process of being dismantled where it stood by the firm of Cashmore's. The locomotive had probably suffered a serious failure rendering it unsuitable for being towed to a distant scrapyard. A rather sad end for a locomotive that was less than 12 years old with plenty of years left in it, had it been permitted a proper lifespan. *Tom Curtis*

together with maximum running speed. Typically halts were made, where convenient, every 25 miles or so and the train, which was classed as an 'Out of Gauge Load', was restricted to a maximum running speed of 25mph. A small tag would be tied to the locomotive's handrail recording the purchaser and destination. If a brake van was not provided then the provision of a 'rider' for one or more of the locomotives was deemed necessary whose job it was to operate the engine's handbrake to give additional braking power when required. Vacuum-braked wagons might also be included in the train, again to provide additional braking power, the maximum load permitted for a dead engine movement being four locomotives. The pages of the railway journals of the time are littered with sightings of these melancholy processions and the occasional report of a 'hot box' or other breakdown which caused the offending locomotive to be detached and parked in a convenient siding until it could be collected.

Typical prices for locomotives were approximately £1500 for a small tank engine and approximately £2–2,500 for a mainline express example. One example, where carriage was paid by BR, shows that in 1966 a 'Merchant Navy' could be had for £2,015 whilst surprisingly a Standard Class 3 tank was only £10 less and an Ivatt tank came in at £1,300. Where carriage was at the expense of the contractor, typical total sums charged were £1,630 for a Standard Class 5 from Nine Elms to Newport, £1,756 for an 'S15' from Feltham to Newport and £1,430 for a

'Q1' from Eastleigh to Morriston. The sale by BR was on the understanding that 'locos and tenders will be broken up'. This was subsequently rescinded such that re-sale of locomotives was only permitted by a scrapyard subject to a levy placed upon the sale. Woodham's for example set the price for each locomotive at its exact scrap value (each type had an exact metal content breakdown from BR, so this was simply taken and multiplied by that day's scrap rate for each metal component), plus the BR levy, with the sale price completed by the addition of VAT, initially set at 10% but raised to 15% in 1979. For most of the time that locomotives were being 'rescued' from Barry it became accepted commercial practice by the scrap merchant for preservation groups to pay a deposit for a particular locomotive, which then achieved 'protected/reserved' status until the group could pay for the locomotive in full and arrange transport. In practice this meant that parts continued to be stolen, the large site being very open and insecure. Other sites were more protected, often by high fencing, spotlights and even guard dogs. An offer was apparently made to Derby, who controlled the tendering and disposal of redundant BR rolling stock, to purchase one of the trio of 'Schools' located at the Cransley site. However, at the time Cohen's, like other scrap dealers who bought BR locomotives, were prohibited from selling on the 4-4-0 to preservationists as their contract with BR prohibited sale to third parties. It is not known which of the 'Schools' was the subject of this appeal but back in late 1963 the *Railway*

Observer had reported, erroneously as it turned out, that 30902 *Wellington* had been purchased for preservation by a businessman in the Isle of Man. Apparently the locomotive was originally intended to go to the Railway Preservation Society's site at Hednesford Staffordshire but due to lack of space it was to join 46201 *Princess Elizabeth* at the Dowty site at Ashchurch until more suitable accommodation could be found. Nothing more was heard of this scheme and by the middle of the following year the three 'Schools' had met their fate at Cransley.

Locomotives could often be seen in the BR sidings at Kettering or on Kettering shed where foreign locomotives looked very much out of place amongst the local '8Fs' and '4F's then still allocated there, awaiting the trip up the spur line to Cransley, especially if Cohen's own sidings were fully occupied. Stock would often have taken some time just to arrive at Kettering, either from their home depots or from various BR collection yards. This was not

just a reflection of the length of journey involved but also the state of the locomotive in question for often 'hot boxes' or similar ailments would require sidelining or attention en route thus delaying transit. A case in point was Maunsell 'W' class tank 31924 which was despatched from London's Nine Elms depot in October 1964 and was subsequently noted on Wellingborough shed on 8 November. It had only moved as far as Kettering shed yard two weeks later, 22 November, where it was noted alongside ex GWR '72xx' 2-8-2T 7218. In some cases, however, the journey could be interrupted by the attitude of staff operating the relevant freight working, as happened on 27 September 1969 when a trio of 'Black 5s' which were en route to Cohen's at Kettering was halted at New Mills near Gowhole when the driver reckoned his eight hours duty was up and refused to take the train any further. The consist was consequently parked in the up goods loop. After being left here for more than a month,

A common sight in the mid 1960s when it seemed as if every available yard and siding was filled with redundant rolling stock. Bulleid 'Q1' 33024, which had been withdrawn in August 1963, in company with Standard tank 80084 and 'K' Mogul 32343, are pictured with tell-tale sacking over their chimneys parked in a siding at Three Bridges awaiting their sale to various scrap merchants. The 'Q1' was to end up at Cohen's in Cransley along with three other examples of its classmates, the 'K' went to King's of Norwich in October 1964 almost two years after its withdrawal in November 1962, whilst the Standard tank was dealt with by Bird's at Morriston.

suffering the attentions of local vandals, the locomotives were pronounced unfit to move until inspected by the C&W (Carriage & Wagon) Department. On 6 December a couple of them were finally shifted leaving one remaining – it was still there a month later! Not all movements were long distance however, witness the transfer of Ivatt Mogul 46495 which had spent most of its life allocated to Kettering depot 15B. Locomotives tended to arrive in batches rather than as singletons such as occurred on 1 October 1967 when several ex LMS (London, Midland & Scottish) 2-6-4Ts including Fairburn tank 42233 were noted in the reception sidings.

The end of 1962 had seen withdrawal en bloc of the last members of Maunsell's 4-4-0s, amongst the last of them being 30902 *Wellington*, 30921 *Shrewsbury* and 30935 *Sevenoaks* from Nine Elms depot. They proved to be surprising arrivals at Cransley on 24 March 1964 hauled by a Stanier '8F'. Previously three 'S15s', 30497/30509/30514, were towed from Feltham shed on 19 March and the following day a 'W' tank and an 'H16' and a 'Q1', 31922/30518/33002, also arrived. On 23 March a 'Q1', 33013 in steam, brought up a further 'Q1' and an 'S15', 33008 and 30507, and all were to become local celebrities being considered 'foreigners'

amongst the railway fraternity. They were to be much photographed in the yard in various stages of demolition. On 13 April 'Q1s' 33016/33024 and stovepipe chimneyed 'Q' class 30549 were noted passing Bedford Midland en route to Kettering. These movements, often from the SR collection point at Feltham depot, were operated as Class 8 freights. It was usual for the engine scrap tonnage to be painted on the locomotives but at Cohen's this was also painted on the tenders where appropriate with 'S15' 30507 for example displaying the figures '92T'. The method of scrapping was generally left to the individual gangs concerned, some preferring to start with the cab and working forward whilst others attacked the front end initially, although generally the valuable firebox was left until last. Tenders were often dealt with separately and marshalled with redundant brakevans on a siding leading towards Loddington. It was thought at one time that nothing less than a 'Merchant Navy' might be destined for Cohen's as '8F' 48197 towed in a fresh arrival to Kettering on 28 September in the shape of 35002 *Union Castle*. However the 'Merchant' was only stopping off on its journey to its ultimate resting place, the gloriously named Slag Reduction Co. of Rotherham, where it met its end together with classmate 35015 *Rotterdam Lloyd*.

Redundant LT stock is being hauled through Maidenhead by Class 47 No. 47 244 en route to the Long Marston scrapyard of Bird's on 26 May 1977 *Peter Robins*

2
Scrapyards

Breakers' yards have always exerted a fascination on railway enthusiasts who wished to take a last look at their favourite locomotives before they were reduced to lumps of scrap. Some were easier to access than others but perhaps the most famous, and certainly one of the most accessible, was that of Woodham Brothers at Barry in South Wales. They were noted not for the volume of locomotives dealt with but for the fact that over 200 were ultimately saved as the attention of the scrapmen there turned elsewhere to the volume of withdrawn wagons that the yard handled. The 'Top Ten' locomotive scrapyards in the UK, which each dealt with hundreds of disposals, comprised Cashmore of Great Bridge, Tipton and Newport, Bird at Risca, Buttigieg also in Newport,

The spectacular Barry panorama which revealed line after line of rusting hulks, the majority of which, against all expectations, would go on to be rescued in subsequent years by a wide variety of preservation societies.

'Merchant Navy' No. 35012 *United States Line* in company with 'West Country' No. 34044 *Woolacombe* awaits entry into Cashmore's yard Newport on 22 October 1967. *Derek Jones*

Vic Berry's famous Leicester yard with Class 25s awaiting stacking and subsequent disposal, captured at 06:30 on Sunday morning 14 June 1987. *Railphotoprints – Gordon Edgar*

King's of Norwich took a number of ex SR locomotives including this 'K' class Mogul No. 32337 seen on 25 April 1964. *Norfolk Railway Society Collection – Roger Harrison*

the Central Wagon Co. at Ince, Drapers of Hull, Hughes Bolckow of North Blyth, Motherwell Machinery of Wishaw and Thomas Ward located at Beighton and at Killamarsh near Sheffield. Other firms which played a major role in disposing of the BR fleet included Arnott Young with yards in Glasgow and Rotherham, Barnes & Bell of Coatbridge, Campbell of Airdrie and Shieldhall, Connell of Coatbridge, Coopers Metals at Sharpness, Hayes of Bridgend, King of Norwich, Loom (Ellis Metals) of Spondon, McLellan of Bo'ness and Glasgow, McWilliam of Shettleston, Settle Speakman of Queenborough, Shipbreaking Industries of Faslane, Thomas Ward of Wishaw and the subject of this volume, George Cohen.

3

The Firm of George Cohen

George Cohen, Sons and Company was a scrap metal merchant with offices at 600 Commercial Road, London E14. The company was founded by George Henry Cohen, who died in 1890, as Messrs. George Cohen & Co. in 1834 and changed its name in 1883 on the appointment of the son of the founder Michael Cohen. After the First World War the company won a number of large contracts to dispose of the vast supplies of surplus munitions including 400,000 tons of high explosives and other shells. In 1940 the company moved its head offices to Hammersmith. The company also got involved in demolition work with projects such as the towers of Crystal Palace, which had survived the great fire, and the Dome of Discovery and the Skylon which had been erected for the Festival of Britain in 1951. They also helped to recover the infrastructure of London's tram system which finally closed in the following year, and were instrumental in the scrapping of London's last trams at Penhall Road between July 1952 and January 1953. The breaking of these trams involved attaching to the tramcar body a steel hawser fixed to a tractor and pulling it off its bogies. Cohen's were to deal with a quantity of

Below and opposite Two views of the scrapping operation undertaken at the rear of Colindale depot by George Cohen between 1959 and 1962. Trolleybuses featured are FXH 426 below with, opposite, a general view of the quagmire which the yard became after heavy rain, with more than a dozen examples awaiting the end. *Both Bob Martin*

withdrawn trolley buses, at the rear of Colindale depot, following withdrawal of London's trolleybus services between 1959 and 1962. A short film featuring this activity, entitled *Trolleybus Breakup,* is available to view on the Pathe website www.britishpathe.com.

In 1956 a holding company, The George Cohen 600 Group Limited, was formed to control the original company together with its many subsidiaries. The '600 Group' name, derived from the company's first address, had been used informally since the Second World War. In 1970 the '600 Group' set up a joint venture, Six Hundred Metal Holdings, with Thorn Electrical Industries to operate the two companies' metal-handling businesses. 1975 saw the company name change to The 600 Group Limited and in 1981 a further name change was made to The 600 Group plc. In 1987 George Cohen, Sons and Company was renamed GCS (Steels) Limited, part of the 600 Group. The scrap metal business was acquired by Monks Ferry (Ship Breaking) Ltd. of St. Helens near Warrington in Merseyside. The head office of GCS Steels was based at Stanningley Works in Leeds. This site covering some 14 acres with its own shunting line to transport large quantities of steel products operated until closure in 1999. In 2013 GCS Steels became a subsidiary of Pyramid Trading Limited.

Although this volume focuses upon the Cohen's operation at Cransley they did have other scrapping locations across the UK which witnessed some notable steam departures such as 'A4' 60002 *Sir Murrough*

Wilson which arrived at their Cargo Fleet site in October 1964 directly from store at Heaton MPD (Motive Power Depot). Their operation at Tinsley Sheffield first came to notice in September 1962 when 'J26' 65773 was spotted in pieces in the yard; it is believed that this locomotive may have arrived semi-cut from Darlington Works. During the next five years locomotives arrived at Tinsley, never in appreciable numbers, and they tended to be of the smaller types such as LMS '4F', '2F', '1F' and '0F' classes including 47002/8/9 0-4-0STs and 47164 Fowler '2F' Dock Tank. Perhaps their most notable victim was named 'B1' 61249 *FitzHerbert Wright*. The last locomotive recorded at Tinsley was '3F' 47534 in November 1967. Their Morriston, near Swansea, operation took no less than 98 ex GWR (Great Western Railway) types, mostly coming from local Welsh sheds, including 8 'Castles' and 12 'Halls'. Mogul 5336, the last survivor of the series, also went to the Morriston site as did 29 Ivatt tanks including the ex Somerset & Dorset examples. Occasionally parts were salvaged from locomotives and used to assist in restorations elsewhere as happened with Cransley's '8F' 48467 which in February 1969 carried on its side a message to the effect that spares would be taken to help in the restoration of sister locomotive 48773 based on the Severn Valley Railway at Bridgnorth. Cohen's also had a site at Ickles near Rotherham which saw off some 40 locomotives, at Kingsbury near Birmingham which handled less than a dozen and at South Bank Middlesbrough which handled a similar small number. Following the end of steam withdrawals Cohen's

The last depot to operate trolleybuses was Fulwell and prominent in this view taken at the rear of Colindale depot in 1962 is 'L3' class No. 1499, still carrying its Fulwell depot plate, whilst on the left is No. 1641. *Geoff Plumb*

SCRAP
IRON & STEEL
NON-FERROUS
Scrap METALS

WORKS PURCHASED
for
DISMANTLING
and
DEMOLITION

GEORGE COHEN
SONS AND CO. LTD.
600 Commercial Rd. London. E.14
'Phone: STEpney Green 3434
And at LEEDS. BIRMINGHAM. SHEFFIELD
MANCHESTER. NEWCASTLE. GLASGOW etc

continued to buy stock from BR in the diesel era although the majority of diesel locomotives were scrapped by BR themselves from the late 1970s onwards with just a few major yards like Cohen's, Booth's and Slag Reduction taking any appreciable numbers and even then they accounted for generally less than 100 apiece. Of course freight stock, mainly carriages in Cransley's case, continued to provide much scrapping work as the older types of vehicle were withdrawn. Several industrial locomotives were retained for internal shunting use and for subsequent resale.

The futuristic 'Skylon' exhibited at the 1951 Festival of Britain was recovered for scrap by Cohen's

With top decks and lower deck side panels removed these two examples are nearing the end of the road. London Transport trolleybuses finished running on 8 May 1962 and this picture, taken in about July 1962, captures their last moments at Colindale depot yard. *Geoff Plumb*

4

Cransley Ironworks &
The Loddington Branch

Cohen's yard near Kettering was situated on the site of Coburn Works, the former Cransley ironstone furnaces where ore was smelted to make pig iron. The first two furnaces were put into blast in 1877 with a third added in 1882 and they were operated by the New Cransley Iron & Steel Co. from 1889. The growth of the Northamptonshire iron ore extraction industry which began about 1850 sparked the building of local ironworks and rail systems to serve them. The Cransley & Loddington line was unique in that it was promoted by a mainline railway company rather than the quarry operators. The Midland Railway branch of 1¼ miles in length was built from Kettering to Cransley and opened in 1877 to serve the ironworks, the quarries being some distance away from the works and served by a 2ft 6in tramway.

In order to serve the quarries better the MR extended their line by some two miles in 1893 although metre-gauge tramways continued to serve the extremities of the line as the site of extraction was constantly changing as reserves became exhausted. Mechanised extraction of ore, using steam powered excavators, began in 1909 and some of these machines could still be seen lying derelict on site into the 1950s. Plans to extend the line further in 1941 came to nothing although conversion from metre to standard gauge did take place at the ends of the line. Stewarts & Lloyds took over the operation in 1956 but closure of the furnaces came on 1 November 1959. Two factors militated against the economics of smelting here, the rather low grade of the ore and the distance required to transport it from the quarries which served it. Both the neighbouring furnaces at Kettering and Islip did not suffer from these problems. Demolition followed in 1960 but the ore bunkers remained on site until at least 1962. In 1960 negotiations had been opened with Cohen's for use of the site for metal scrap recovery. The old ironworks site was located one mile west of Kettering station to which it was connected by a single-track railway, part of the former Loddington ironstone quarry branch which closed to regular traffic in June 1963 upon closure of the quarries. When Cohen's took over the site

A view of the former Cransley Ironworks site which became the home of Cohen's scrapyard in 1963.

The former running shed at Cransley housed a couple of industrial locomotives, formerly used by the Cransley Iron & Steel Co., at the time that Cohen's took over the site. They inherited this pair of saddle tanks which they duly went on to scrap in March 1966. Leading this view is Peckett 0-4-0ST No. 832 dating from 1900. The locomotive was built for Huntley & Palmers of Reading, where it was known as locomotive D, and is commemorated in a Hornby OO model where it is finished in the attractive blue livery of the biscuit manufacturer. No. 832 went through the hands of a number of industrial concerns before ending up at Cransley.

The other occupant of the shed at Cransley was this altogether rarer Chapman & Furneaux 0-4-0ST built at their Gateshead works in 1900. It was one of only about 70 locomotives that the firm constructed and one of only two examples to work in the East Midlands ironstone area. It was named *New Cransley No. 3*, the rusty patch on the tanks indicating the former position of the nameplate. The locomotive was rebuilt in 1952 at the Holywell Works. Chapman & Furneaux ceased trading in 1902, their goodwill being taken over by Hawthorn Leslie& Co.

(27105)
British Railways Board (H)
West Midlands Branch
Railway Correspondence & Travel Society
South Midlands Rail Tour
Saturday 18th May, 1968
Rugby, Northampton, Hardingstone Junction,
Blisworth, Leighton Buzzard, Worcester Curve,
Bedford No. 1, Higham Ferrers, Loddington,
Islip Sidings, Market Harborough,
Northampton, Rugby
SECOND CLASS   For conditions see over

0040   0040

One of the few railtours to traverse the Loddington branch was this RCTS special of 18 May 1968 which originated at Rugby and utilised a three-car DMU. In spite of reports in the Railway Observer that passengers would not be welcome in the yard this is photographic evidence that tour participants did indeed detrain to inspect the stock. *RCTS Archive*

Seen inside the shed at Loddington on 13 February 1966 is one of two Hawthorn Leslie 0-6-0STs, works numbers 3883/4 dating from 1936, obtained in 1957 from the Appleby Frodingham Steel Co. The pair were practically identical and both were given the same livery, the only appreciable difference between them was the chimney, HL3884 retaining the original chimney whilst HL3883 had a slender chimney. Although the quarry had officially closed in 1963 there were rumours, as late as 1965, of a possible re-opening but this never materialised. The two Hawthorn Leslie locomotives, named *New Cransley No. 3* and *No. 7*, were cut up here by Cohen's in September 1966.

Below Also in the shed was *William Ellis*, an Avonside metre-gauge 0-6-0ST. The cab had been cut back to enable it to pass under a bridge by the terminus but unfortunately this did not enhance its looks. Behind it is No. 3884 which had been resting on the wooden blocks seen here since 1963. This locomotive was cut up here by Cohen's in May 1966. *All Derek Fear*

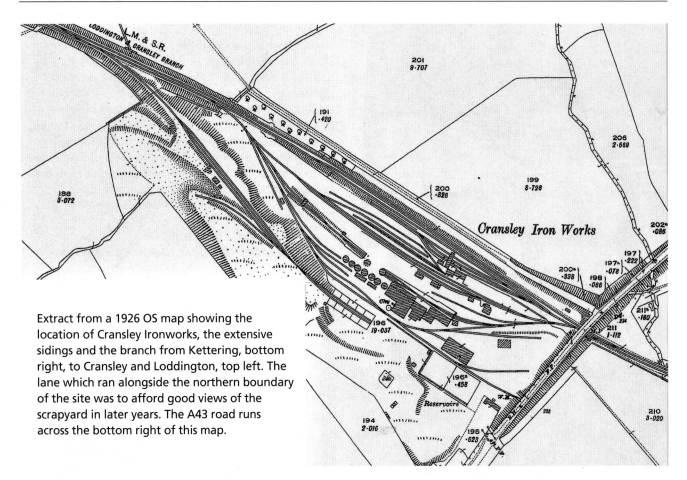

Extract from a 1926 OS map showing the location of Cransley Ironworks, the extensive sidings and the branch from Kettering, bottom right, to Cransley and Loddington, top left. The lane which ran alongside the northern boundary of the site was to afford good views of the scrapyard in later years. The A43 road runs across the bottom right of this map.

they inherited two locomotives parked in the shed at Cransley which they subsequently scrapped. These were an unnamed and unnumbered 0-4-0ST Peckett Works No. 832 built in 1900, formerly of Gibbs and Canning Ltd Wilnecote, and an unusual Chapman & Furneaux 0-4-0ST of 1900 formerly named *New Cransley No. 3* from nearby Loddington Quarries. This was one of only two Chapman & Furneaux locomotives to work in the East Midlands ironstone quarries.

The line to Loddington was retained for a number of years in the expectation that the quarries might re-open and indeed an RCTS (Railway Correspondence & Travel Society) diesel multiple unit (DMU) special traversed the branch in May 1968. The special passed Cohen's site but as reported in *Railway Observer*: 'Advance notice had been given that the party would not be welcome in the scrapyard and a reception party of two men and a dog awaited our arrival. Serious confrontation was however avoided as a shower of rain intervened at the crucial moment. Seventeen BR locomotives were noted in the yard (15 steam and 2 diesel) as well as 21 tenders, a number of brakevans, and 3 of Cohen's own locomotives.' However, this did not apparently prevent the DMU from stopping at the site and the tour participants from detraining as illustrated above. Cohen's site was not visible from the mainline but a convenient farm track that led off the A43 ran alongside the full length of the yard affording a grandstand view of proceedings. One generally thinks of scrapyards as being located deep in the urban landscape often surrounded by scenes of dereliction but pictures of

Cohen's yard at Cransley surprisingly show that the site was surrounded by green fields, trees and hedgerows strangely out of keeping with scenes of dismemberment of locomotive carcasses that went on there. Overlooked by the spoil heap of the former ironworks new sidings were laid in by the Eagre Construction Ltd. in the summer of 1962 to accommodate the redundant stock bought from BR by Cohen's who began operations here in January 1963. Eagre Construction were later involved in the lifting of the former S&MJR (Stratford-upon-Avon & Midland Junction Railway) line from Blisworth Ironstone Sidings to Woodford West Junction and recovery of sidings at Woodford Halse in the mid 1960s. They were also responsible for lifting the former LNWR (London & North Western Railway) line from Banbury to Verney Junction in 1967. They used an 0-6-0DM John Fowler locomotive Works No. 22885/1940 on these contracts. Initially steam locomotives from Kettering shed and latterly Type 2 diesels were used to trip withdrawn stock down the branch from Kettering. Officially BR was only required by the terms of their scrap contracts to deliver stock to the entrance to Cohen's sidings whence the scrap merchants own internal shunting locomotives would position stock. However, on occasions a backhander to BR crews would no doubt have saved the yard the trouble of starting up the engine of their own shunter!

Interest in the yard by enthusiasts was sparked off by a local newspaper article published in April 1964 which mentioned that cutting of redundant steam locomotives was now occurring at a site at Cransley. Demand for

Two scrapyard views, dating from 10 May 1978, with Class 25 No. 25056 on the thrice weekly freight service which took away loaded scrap from Cransley. Note the hut in the foreground of the second image which is also evident in the earlier view seen on page 18. Cohen's own shunter is also present amongst the debris and it will be noted in this first view that the track has been recovered on the former route to Loddington. *Both Lewis Bevan*

End of the line for the scrapyard.

local ore reduced in the 1960s and the branch closed to normal traffic in July 1963. Track beyond Cohen's site was maintained on an 'out of use' basis should demand for local ore revive. June 1970 saw the line taken out of use formally beyond Cohen's site. The line to Cohen's remained officially open until October 1980. The yard was cleared by September the following year and was later used as a car breaking yard. The sidings at Cransley and the remainder of the branch to Kettering were lifted within a couple of years. Road improvements to the A43 and construction of the A14 since closure have severed the route in two places between Kettering and Cransley. The old scrapyard site was taken over as a car breaker's yard until 2007 and once this enterprise had finished stories were told of excavations amongst the rubble revealing parts of locomotives which it was hoped would produce some lucrative scrap sales but the more sinister discovery of blue asbestos taken from locomotive boiler cladding and dumped down a bank at the rear of the site caused excavations to be hastily aborted and infilled. Military hardware and Victorian glassware in the shape of sought after bottles were also to be found on occasions. The site lay dormant for a number of years and was cleared of debris and industrial contamination left over from the ironworks furnace and subsequent scrapping operations. Infrastructure for the future use of the site was completed in 2011. The 32-acre site adjacent to junction 8 of the A14 is being advertised as Cransley Park and in 2016 the site owners, the St Francis Group, submitted a planning application seeking detailed consent to build five new industrial units.

The site was originally granted outline planning consent for up to 41,790sq m (450,000sq ft) of development comprising B2 Industrial use, B8 Storage and Distribution use and C1 Hotel use in 2006 but the onset of the recession in 2008 postponed any activity on the site. Beyond Cransley, although the trackbed of the former railway can be walked in many places, much hard evidence of the Northamptonshire ironstone industry has, as elsewhere in the county, been erased from the landscape. So it is that all traces of this fascinating former scrapyard have been lost and only those haunting images of stock being reduced

to scrap amongst unexpectedly bucolic surroundings, that were very foreign to the former homes of many of the locomotives being despatched, will remain to remind us of the railway graveyard that was once situated here.

The Millennium Sculpture sited in Great Cransley was fabricated by the James Brothers, blacksmiths of Broughton, and was made from iron reclaimed from the old Cransley furnaces. It contains seven plaques which depict the history of the parish and the sculpture was erected in 2000 from local subscriptions and donations made in the parish. One of the plaques depicts Cransley furnaces which were built in the 1890s to remove iron from the locally mined iron ore. This new local industry saved the Cransley estate from bankruptcy as it had been on the market since 1884 and was not sold until 1903 when the iron revenues began to flow.

What it all comes down to in the end – nothing more than assorted parts. Cylinder blocks which once provided propulsion now lie in heaps, their power all spent. Notice the scrapman perched precariously in the far left of the top view in those far off days before Health & Safety made its mark. *David Hills*

5

Comings and Goings at Cransley

The pages of the *Railway Observer* magazine published by the RCTS gave details of the arrival of locomotives, their last shed, thereby indicating distance travelled to Cransley, and by inference their length of stay in the yard, and subsequent despatch. A review of the entries for 1967 for example reveals the following information.

The following were delivered to Cohen's yard from Kettering for cutting –
43018, 48514, 48527 – 26 January
46495, 47384, 47397, 47482, 47494, 47530, 47615, 47649 – 27 January
47318, 47396, 47435, 48755, 92013 – 31 January
3605 – 2 February
Sold to Cohen's Kettering in January – 44678 (Springs Branch)

At Cransley on 11 February 3605, 43018, 46519, 47318, 47396, 47397, 47435, 47482, 47530, 47649, 47658, 48225, 48514, 48527, 48755, 92013 and on 20 January 47521 arrived.
Sold to Cohen's Kettering in February/March – 3607 (Saltley), 47410, 47437 (Nuneaton), 48088 (Buxton), 48372 (Newton Heath), 44773 (Edge Hill), 44834, 45071 (Speke Junction).
Sold to Cohen's Kettering in April – 48270 (Kirkby)

At Cransley on 4 April were – 3605, 43018, 47318, 47396, 47435, 48270, 48514, 48527, 48755, 92013
Sold to Cohen's Kettering in June – 48536 (Speke Junction), 48739 (Lostock Hall)
Sold to Cohen's Kettering in August – 42086, 42133 (Birkenhead), 42224 (Lostock Hall), 45109 (Warrington), 76041, 76095 (Chester)
Sold to Cohen's Kettering in September/October – 44696, 44870 (Newton Heath), 45343 (Rose Grove), 43129 (Normanton), 43130, 44695, 44853, 48542 (Wakefield), 45303 (Newton Heath), 48162, 48202, 48394 (Royston).
Sold to Cohen's Kettering in November – 44659, 44768, 45069, 92103 (Speke Junction), 45040, 45071 (Crewe), 45191, 45302 (Stoke), 76008 (Salisbury).
Sold to Cohen's Kettering in December – 44821, 45278, 45308, 92100 (Crewe), 45057, 45242, 45412 (Speke Junction), 45256 (Warrington).

At Cransley on 29 November were –ED3, 42267, 43129, 43130, 44659, 44661, 44695, 44696, 44768, 44821, 44870, 44930, 45003, 45019, 45024, 45050, 45069, 45071, 45191, 45278, 45302, 45303, 45308, 45343, 48256, 48542, 76008, 76041, 76095, 92090, 92100, 92103.

From the above it can be seen that the majority of locomotives arriving at Cransley at this time had been withdrawn from the North West consisting mainly of 'Black 5s' and Stanier '8Fs' with just one Standard Class 4 from the Southern Region at Salisbury. A comparison of sightings in the yard shows that, for example, 43018 arrived on 26 January, was noted in the yard on 11 February was still there on 4 April but had been despatched by 29 November. It might take a few weeks between date of sale and arrival at Kettering and the length of stay in the yard varied but cutting was usually undertaken within three months or so of arrival, for example 48536 and 48739 were sold to Cohen's in June but had been scrapped by the time of the visit on 29 November and 76041 sold in

August was, as might be expected, still there at the end of November. However this was not a hard and fast rule and depended upon the rate of scrapping, workforce available, other stock to be cut, etc. These sales and movements should be taken as a rough guide only as locomotives are mentioned in sighting data that have not previously been mentioned in sales information, thus raising questions about the comprehensiveness of the information ,dependent as it was upon the submission by correspondents to the magazine. The What Really Happened to Steam (WRHTS) project aims to produce comprehensive lists of locomotives scrapped at various locations correcting errors previously shown in the 'What happened to Steam' publications by Peter Hands. Details of their progress can be found on their website.

In July 1965 the *RO* (*Railway Observer*) listed those locomotives sold so far to date at Cransley on a month by month basis –

March 1964	30497/30507/30509/30514/30902/30921/30925/33002
April 1964	30518/30549/31922/33013/33016/33024
August 1964	3852/6839/41326/41327/44109/44171/44492/44540
October 1964	44191/44380
November 1964	3622/4649/6808/7218/7431/31912/31914/31924/41228/41712/43928/43951/44182/44441/ 44529/44572/44577/44581/82011/82012/82013/82014
December 1964	43988/44244/44260/47355
January 1965	47501
February 1965	44575
March 1965	92036

Diesel observations were also made from time to time and the following were noted in the yard on 15 June 1969 –

D2176, D3637, D8202, D8213, D8223, D8227, D8235, D8236, D8238, D8240, D8400, D8401, D8402, D8405, D8407, 12124

The *RO* also lists details of rolling stock which was sold by BR and moved to scrapyards. Review of the *RO* for 1971 for example reveals the following sales and movements in relation to Cohen's at Cransley –

Moved from Yarmouth to Cohen's Kettering November 1970 – E15077
E43127 sold to Cohen's Kettering February 1971
M79610 had been moved to Kettering, presumably for Cohen's, by 27 February 1971
Condemned at Kettering, presumably for Cohen's, M15234/45, 15828, 24210, 24403, 24539, 24651 – 28 February 1971
M56211, E79025, M79119/21/23/27/29/80, M79610/33/40/72/78 at Cohen's Kettering on 7 March 1971
M15234/45, M15395, E15479, E15641, E24311/48, E24401/3, E25095, E43009, E43175 at Cohen's Kettering 28 March 1971
Colchester to Kettering 7 July – E9328, 24665, 34328
Micheldever to Kettering 25 August S96361/73-75/84/88, 96401/02/12 with non standards S3729/30S (SCV), M32959, 33018, 37939M and departmental DS70178, 70216. It is presumed the horseboxes are now condemned, having been officially stored at Micheldever for some time.
Colchester to Kettering 7 July – E3, 9077, 13886, 70003E, DE320583, 320666.

6
BR Steam Locomotives Scrapped at Cransley – Western Region

One of the nine pannier tanks, from two different classes, to end up in the yard is this example of the '5700' class No. 3605 which was photographed on a chilly but bright Sunday morning in March 1967. Hailing from Oxley shed, No. 3605 was withdrawn in September 1966 after a working life of 27 years. *John Evans*

During its final months in service numberless pannier tank No. 3605 shuffles about the yard at Bilston West in 1965. *Brian Robbins Railphotoprints*

No 3607 was one of two long-serving Worcester-based pannier tanks that were present in the yard on 5 March 1967. The pre 1957 BR totem featuring the 'cycling lion' can just be made out on the tank underneath all that grime. Unusually the coupling rods were still in situ and not tied onto the running plate as was often the case. *John Evans*

The appearance of '2800' class 2-8-0 No. 3852 has been freshened up by a recent rain shower on 11 October 1964. *Transport Treasury – Eric Sawford*

The gaunt remains of former '5700' class 0-6-0PT No. 4649 are seen on 29 November 1964. *Transport Treasury – Eric Sawford*

The sole representative of the elegant 'Castle' class to grace the Cransley site was No. 5018 *St. Mawes Castle* which had been withdrawn from Reading shed at the end of April 1964. It is captured in this view, taken on 24 May 1964, being one of the first arrivals at Cohen's. It keeps strange company here with a 'Schools' class and redundant LT Underground stock. The loss of its safety valve bonnet had occurred whilst it was still in service as depicted in the following image. *Transport Treasury – Leslie Freeman*

Photographic evidence that No. 5018 ran in service without its safety valve cover is apparent in this view of the locomotive as it approaches Westbury with a service from Reading in May 1963 during what would be its final 12 months in service. *Railphotoprints collection*

Little room left for doubting the identity of this Collett '5600' lass 0-6-2T as someone has taken the trouble to emblazon the smokebox door with the stencilled number 6656. Withdrawn from Stourbridge Junction shed at the end of September 1965, after a creditable 37 years' service, the locomotive is seen here on a snowy 13 February 1966. *Derek Fear*

A brace of 'Granges' sit out the wintry snow showers in February 1966. The leading locomotive is No. 6853 *Morehampton Grange* latterly a Tyseley based locomotive which had been withdrawn at the end of October 1965. Note the dog taking an interest – was this part of Cohen's security or just a passing stray? *Derek Fear*

Above No. 6928 *Underley Hall* was to be the only example of this class to meet its end at Cransley. It is seen here on 3 October 1965 with its identity chalked on the front bufferbeam and cabside. *Transport Treasury – Eric Sawford*

Below Standing on the running line amongst the recent arrivals at the yard and photographed on 29 November 1964 was this '7200' class No. 7218 withdrawn from Banbury shed at the end of September 1964 having completed almost 30 years of service. *Transport Treasury – Eric Sawford*

With Standard Class 3 tank No. 82011, late of Nine Elms depot, for company '7400' class pannier tank No. 7431 is in residence having journeyed all the way from Wrexham's Croes Newydd shed. The pair is seen on 13 December 1964.
Transport Treasury – Eric Sawford

End of the Line for the 'Granges'

The GWR '6800' or 'Grange' class was a mixed traffic 4-6-0 built to replace the '4300' class 2-6-0. All 80 of the class were constructed at Swindon Works utilising some reconditioned parts from withdrawn '4300' class locomotives. Between 1936 and 1939 100 of the '4300' class were taken out of service and stripped of parts. The initial plan was to build 80 'Grange 'class and 20 'Manor' class thus replacing all 100 of the '4300' class but the onset of the Second World War halted the programme. They proved to be reliable in service even though they were built to a 35-year-old design and proved their capability in handling most duties on the network. Their smaller driving wheels gave them a higher tractive effort than the 'Hall' class and they were often used for the haulage of perishable goods, such as fruit and broccoli, and for excursion trains. Their power classification was 5MT and route availability colour code was red. They also

No. 6853 *Morehampton Grange* displays its inner workings in this scrapyard view dating from 20 March 1966. *John Evans*

deputised for more powerful locomotives on such prestige turns as the up 'Red Dragon' as far as Cardiff and the 'Cambrian Coast Express' between Wolverhampton and Shrewsbury. They were also useful in performing piloting turns over the notorious South Devon inclines. Those based at Banbury shed also handled intermediate legs of the York–Bournemouth through trains.

October 1960 saw the first 'Grange' condemned, 6801 of Penzance shed, and it was cut up at Swindon which was to go on to despatch 15 of the class in total. A further two examples were withdrawn in 1961 with just one going in 1962 and five in 1963. The pace of scrapping picked up in 1964 with 26 making their way to the breaker's yard leaving 25 to be disposed of in 1965 in what was supposed to be the final year of steam on the Western Region. The final pair 6849 *Walton Grange* and 6872 *Crawley Grange* was withdrawn from Oxford shed on 31 December 1965, being sold to Cashmore's at Newport. Of the outside scrap merchants, Cashmore's at Newport took the largest number at 12 but Cohen's at Kettering surprisingly handled no less than 10 coming mostly from depots at Oxley and Tyseley although one, 6844, hailed all the way from Llanelli. Cohen's other yard at Kingsbury also took four examples. Oxley shed, coded 84B until 1963 thence 2B until closure on 1 January 1968, had a number of 'Granges' allocated over the years and the following were withdrawn from the shed during the 1960s – 6803/08/11/23/27/28/30/31/33/39/54/57/70/71. Cransley was to take five from Oxley – 6808/31/33/39/71 – with four examples coming from Tyseley shed.

Although no examples were preserved, 6880 *Betton Grange*, which would have been the next number and name in the originally planned sequence, is currently being built at the Llangollen Railway utilising standardised parts from other ex GWR locomotives together with new-build components. The boiler from 5952 *Cogan Hall* was temporarily fitted to the rolling chassis in November 2016 for exhibition at Warley but this is not the boiler which will grace the finished locomotive. Modified Hall 7927

Willington Hall will be the boiler donor and overhaul of this element will be undertaken at Tyseley Locomotive Works. Completion of the finished locomotive is expected during the latter part of 2018. The copper cap of the

chimney of 6880 comes from 6868 *Penrhos Grange* and this item was donated to the project by the Llangollen GWR Locomotive Group.

The line of the former mineral branch from Loddington to Kettering is on the left passing under the A43 road bridge in the distance. The two sidings on the right house '5600' class No .6656 and the pair of 'Grange' class 4-6-0s seen previously. Note the white painted embellishments of smokebox door hinges and shedcode which adorn the front of No. 6853 which was constructed at Swindon in 1937. *Derek Fear*

Two further examples of the class were to be seen in the yard that February day in 1966, the leading locomotive being No. 6879 *Overton Grange* whilst behind is No. 6855 *Saighton Grange*. They had both been allocated to Tyseley latterly and were withdrawn from there at the end of October 1965. Cohen's were to scrap no fewer than 10 members of this class at Cransley, a figure only surpassed by Cashmore's at Newport. *Derek Fear*

The bleak setting of a scrapyard in winter was made even more so by the dusting of snow coating the tops of the locomotive boilers and the running plates. No 6879 awaits the inevitable end which was to come the following month in March 1966. *Derek Fear*

The three support brackets over the centre driving wheel splasher, which formerly supported the nameplate *Saighton Grange*, are still in situ. Unfortunately none of the class made it into preservation although that situation is currently being addressed through the construction of *Betton Grange* No. 6880 at the Llangollen Railway using donor parts from other locomotives. *Derek Fear*

6855 *Saighton Grange*, a long time Tyseley locomotive, is seen climbing Hatton bank with a heavy summer Saturday load about 1960. *Railphotoprints*

A views taken on 24 January 1965 of the boiler tubes of No. 6808 *Beenham Grange* which are in the process of being removed from the locomotive carcass. *David Hills*

No. 6808 was withdrawn from Oxley shed at the end of August 1964. A plentiful supply of gas cylinders attends the locomotive's last rites. *David Hills*

Resplendent on Westbury depot in May 1963 No. 6853 *Morehampton Grange* looks at its best. It was to be withdrawn from Tyseley in October 1964. *Railphotoprints*

8

BR Steam Locomotives Scrapped at Cransley – Southern Region

Above Four of Maunsell's 'S15' class were dealt with at Cransley. The top view shows No. 30507 waiting its turn on 4 April 1964 alongside some examples of pre 1938 LT Underground stock providing a splash of colour amongst the otherwise drab palette so typical of a scrapyard. No. 30507 had made the journey from Feltham on 23 March hauled dead by 'Q1' class 33013 which also had in its consist classmate 33008. *Ron Fisher*

Below 'S15' No. 30509 had been towed from Feltham on 19 March 1964 in company with classmates 30497 and 30514. Work has obviously already started on cutting the boiler casing revealing the tubes beneath by the time that this shot was taken on 4 April. *Ron Fisher*

With 'Q1' No. 33002 and two 'Schools' visible behind, No 30518, the only Maunsell 'H16' to reach Cransley, heads a line of ex SR locomotives on 4 April 1964. The trio of 'Schools' which ended their days here began their journey from Nine Elms depot and had arrived at Kettering on 24 March hauled by a Stanier '8F'. The 'H16' 4-6-2T had left Feltham shed on 20 March along with 'W' tank No. 31922 and 'Q1' No. 33002. As might be expected the arrival of these somewhat exotic examples of SR motive power, never normally seen in this neck of the woods, caused quite a stir amongst the local Northamptonshire railway fraternity and their arrival even made the pages of the local newspaper. *Ron Fisher*

A further look at 'H16' No. 30518, this time with a couple of Bulleid 'Q1s' and a Maunsell 'W' class ahead of the line. It had been withdrawn from service at Feltham shed at the end of November 1962, as part of the major cull of pre-Grouping steam which occurred at this time, and had spent over a year there before its subsequent sale and transport to Cohen's yard. *Ron Fisher*

A reminder of happier times as No. 30518 hurries through Feltham station with a freight for Feltham yard on 3 November 1956. *Railphotoprints*

Unique stovepipe-chimneyed 'Q' class No 30549, withdrawn in July 1963, was the only member of this 20-strong Maunsell-designed 0-6-0 to reach Cransley. On 13 April 1964 'Q1s' Nos. 33016/33024 together with No. 30549 were noted passing Bedford Midland en route to Kettering shed whence they were tripped down the former Loddington branch to Cohen's site. Again former LT Underground stock provides the background to this view.

One of the greatest losses in the late 1962 cull of pre-Grouping steam on the SR was the withdrawal of the last of the famous 'Schools' class. Three examples were destined for Cohen's and all are seen here in April 1964. Leading the trio here is No. 30902 *Wellington* with No. 30921 *Shrewsbury* and No. 30935 *Sevenoaks* behind. *Ron Fisher*

A close up of the remains of No. 30902 *Wellington* which was built in 1930 and ended its days allocated to Nine Elms depot from where it was withdrawn at the end of December 1962. It was stored at Nine Elms for 15 months until transfer to Cohen's in the spring of 1964.

Although masquerading here as *Guildford* this was in fact No. 30921 *Shrewsbury*, another locomotive to be stored at Nine Elms following withdrawal at the end of 1962. Quite why it received the chalked name 'Guildford' is not clear as it was never allocated to Guildford shed although the 'Schools' class did latterly work through the Surrey city on Reading–Redhill line services.

Basingstoke shed plays host to Nine Elms based 'Schools' class No. 30921 *Shrewsbury* in November 1961.
Railphotoprints – Dave Cobbe collection

Two views of the third of the 'Schools' trio to be seen at Cransley No. 30935 *Sevenoaks* which, like its two companions, was also withdrawn from Nine Elms and had a long wait before eventual sale to Cohen's. *Top Ron Fisher*

Looking quite presentable, both sides of 'W' class No. 31922 are illustrated here in these April 1964 shots heading a line of ex SR locomotives. Four members of this class, which had been used extensively on cross-London and suburban freight duties, were dealt with here, No. 31922 having been withdrawn from service at the end of August 1963. Both *Ron Fisher*

'W' class No. 31924 also looks in reasonable condition and it was a pity that none of these heavy tanks could have been saved for posterity. Latterly they had been used on Fawley oil trains, banking duties between Exeter St Davids and Central stations and on e.c.s. duties between Clapham Junction carriage sidings and Waterloo. The lower picture illustrates the unusual provision of brake blocks on the rear pony truck, in addition to those on the driving wheels, to enhance the locomotive's overall braking abilities.

No. 31924 is seen at rest at Hither Green depot in March 1960. *Railphotoprints – Ian Turnbull*

'Q1' No. 33002, one of the early arrivals, is seen in the yard in quite respectable external condition on 14 April 1964.
Transport Treasury – Stephen Summerson

9

BR Steam Locomotives Scrapped at Cransley – Midland Region

One of the SR's allocation of these useful Ivatt 2-6-2Ts, No. 41326, was based at Brighton shed from September 1961 until May 1964 shortly before the shed closed to steam the following month. Following construction at Derby in 1952 the locomotive had begun its working life far from the SR based in Yorkshire at Skipton shed.

Above One of the famous Johnson '1F' 'Half cabs' was a recent arrival at Cohen's on 29 November 1964. Introduced as long ago as 1878, some 23 survivors from a class of 240 were still working as late as 1958 including No. 41712 which dated from 1880. It was withdrawn from Kirkby in Ashfield depot in September 1964. *Transport Treasury – Eric Sawford*

Below No. 41712 sporting a 16A (Nottingham) shedcode engages in some gentle shunting at Nottingham Midland goods yard in 1960. *Railphotoprints – the late Alan H. Bryant*

There were six examples of these numerous Class 4 2-6-4Ts to be found at Cransley including these two specimens, No. 42083 (upper) and an unidentified example (below). No. 42083 was one of the Fairburn variants dating from 1951, having being built at Brighton Works, and it was withdrawn from Normanton shed as late as the end of October 1967. Forty-one examples were constructed at Brighton Works, two of which survive in preservation currently based on the Lakeside & Haverthwaite Railway. White painted smokebox door hinges still embellish the front of the locomotive below.

No. 42083 is seen outside Normanton shed on 28th. March 1967 displaying the rather crudely painted shedcode 55E on its smokebox door, the original plate having been removed either officially or, more probably, unofficially as a souvenir. *Railphotoprints*

No. 42267 was chosen as the prototype for an OO gauge model produced by Bachmann. The original was constructed at Derby Works in 1947 and withdrawn from Wakefield shed in May 1967.

Above No. 43018 was one of the rather ungracefully nicknamed 'Doodlebugs' or even worse 'Flying Pigs', although more formally known as Ivatt Class 4 2-6-0s, and is seen in the yard during February 1967. Strangely enough this too was chosen to be modelled in OO gauge, albeit with a double chimney, again by the firm of Bachmann. The fitting of double chimneys to the initial 50 members of the class did not improve performance and these were later replaced with a single chimney. Six survivors soldiered on until 1968 the last year of BR steam.

Below Another view of No. 43018 displaying its 5D Stoke painted shed code. Built at Horwich Works in 1948 and allocated at one time to Lancaster, it was to last until October 1966 and is seen here on 5 March 1967. Again the rural nature of the scrapyard is very evident in this view. *John Evans*

Two views, taken in glorious sunshine on 30 May 1966, chronicling the latter stages in the dismemberment of ex Midland '4F' No. 44113. There were no less than 19 examples of this design, dating from 1924 and numbering 580 in total, dealt with by Cohen's at Cransley. No. 44113's final allocation was 16D Westhouses shed whence it was withdrawn in January 1966. *Both Derek Fear*

Displaying the yellow stripe on the cabside, which acted as a reminder to footplate crew that the locomotive was banned from operating under the overhead electric wires south of Crewe and that climbing on the tender might not be a good idea, the condition of No 44577 is in marked contrast to the state of the '4F' illustrated in the previous image as work has yet to commence on the cutting operation. Built in 1939 it spent much of its working life at Nottingham and was withdrawn from there in September 1964. *Keith Partlow*

Unsurprisingly the Stanier 'Black 5s' represented the largest class of locomotives dealt with at Cransley, no less than 73 of the 4-6-0s being scrapped here. No. 44708 hailed from Trafford Park from where it was withdrawn in January 1968.

A view of No. 44768 bereft of its connecting rods. Built in 1947 it had given 20 years of faithful service.

Two 'Black 5s', Nos. 44965 from Bolton and 44851 from Newton Heath Manchester, wait their turn in the queue on 4 August 1968 shortly before the formal end of steam on the BR network. Note the stack of insulated containers to the right which were formerly carried on railway wagons also awaiting attention and indicating the diversity of railway rolling stock handled here. *Derek Fear*

Above A scrawled chalked message on the tender of No. 44816 from the 8F Preservation Society is redolent of the many similar messages that adorned locomotives in Barry scrapyard imploring scavengers not to take parts. Whether they were ever granted their wish is not known although the speed of despatch of locomotives once they were in the yard was acknowledged in the final hope expressed – 'If loco lasts this long !' This view dates from April 1969. *George Woods*

Below No. 44816 is seen on Carnforth ash disposal plant near the ferro-concrete coaling stage on 7 October 1967 in company with a classmate and Derby Sulzer D5096 which was based at Leeds Holbeck at the time. *Railphotoprints – Norman Preedy*

With connecting rods typically lashed to the running plate No. 44860 waits ahead of an unidentified Standard Class 4. A Stoke-based locomotive latterly, it lasted in service until January 1967 and was noted at Stoke in July en route to Kettering.

Separated from their tenders and with boiler lagging draped over the running plates the locomotives in front of 'Black 5' No. 44906 make for a sombre scene on 4 August 1968. Soon to join them, No. 44906 dated from October 1945, being constructed at Crewe Works and lasting in service for some 23 years until March 1968 and withdrawal from Edge Hill shed. Eventually 842 members of this numerous class were constructed with the last few seeing out the end of BR steam in the North West in August 1968. *Derek Fear*

Above The front bogie of No. 45046 appears to be off the rails in this view which illustrates the clean lines of this Stanier workhorse. No. 45046 did not quite make the end of BR steam, being withdrawn at the end of June 1968 from Bolton shed surely with many more years of useful life left.

Below No. 45276 has had its cab already removed as a preliminary to tackling the firebox and boiler. The former Loddington branch seen curving away in the right background was not formally taken out of service until June 1970 although it had only been maintained on an 'out of use' basis since July 1963 in the forlorn hope that the local iron ore industry might experience a revival. *Derek Fear*

Above Our final 'Black 5' image captures No. 45376, one of a number of the class built by Armstrong Whitworth, being completed in June1937. It was withdrawn from Edge Hill depot in April 1967. *Derek Fear*

Below Ivatt Class 2 2-6-0 No 46519 is, believe it or not, wearing unlined green livery having been built at Swindon in 1952. It is seen here on 5 March 1967 in its final hours. Notice one of the rods jammed behind the lubricator. *John Evans*

Two further views of the Ivatt Class 2 design with No. 46519 seen again in the upper image with a hand-painted shedcode which appears to be showing 5E Nuneaton although it ended its days at 5D Stoke. No. 46495, the only other member of the class to be handled here, is seen below in what were its final hours.

Above The next 2 pages feature a selection of colour images of a quartet of the famous 'Jinty' 0-6-0Ts, of which 10 examples ended their days at Cransley. No. 47318 started life in 1926, having been constructed by the North British Locomotive Co. It enjoyed a 40-year innings, much of it spent at nearby Northampton shed, lasting in traffic until October 1966. *John Evans*

Below No 47396, also dating from 1926, was a Vulcan Foundry product and was also withdrawn in October 1966. *John Evans*

Above Next in line was No. 47435, a long-time Cricklewood resident, and it was one of three 'Jinties' awaiting breaking up in the yard on 11 April 1967. *John Evans*

Below This 'Jinty' spent many years based at Stafford and Stoke and it is clearly a long time since it had received a major overhaul and repaint as it still carries the pre-1957 BR emblem. It had been withdrawn the previous October and was photographed on a delightful Spring Sunday morning, 5 March 1967. *John Evans*

Above The Jinty at the rear of this shot, dating from February 1967, is No. 47530 but the identity of the other cannot be established now that it is receiving the attentions of the scrapmen who have a rail-mounted crane to assist in the destruction.

Below No 47658 was just one of the 422 members of the class that were ubiquitous over the Midland system. October 1966 saw its long career come to an end.

Opposite top Stanier '8Fs' were the second largest class represented at Cohen's with 27 examples being despatched at Cransley. Seemingly being overtaken by vegetation this is No. 48514, at one time allocated to Bescot shed, with the rolling fields of Northamptonshire affording a pleasant pastoral backdrop. *John Evans*

Opposite bottom A visit to the scrapyard on 5 March 1967 revealed a batch of engines recently arrived from storage at Tyseley among which was Class 8F 2-8-0 No 48755 with a shed code that indicated she had arrived from 2E. *John Evans*

Above To borrow from J. S. Bach's cantata this shot might well be entitled 'Where sheep may safely graze' as there appears to be a stray flock wandering across the tracks. In the foreground of this April 1969 view stands an '8F' with its cylinders and motion already removed. *George Woods*

Above A hole has been cut in this tender, presumably done to permit easy access to the interior. This view was taken on 5 March 1967. *John Evans*

Below Chimneypiece! *George Woods*

10

BR Steam Locomotives Scrapped at Cransley – Eastern Region

The Eastern was the least represented of the BR regions at Cransley with only 13 locomotives spread between two classes being dealt with here. Eight 'B1s' met their end here including No. 61329 seen on 21 August 1966, having been withdrawn from Doncaster four months previously. Interestingly this was one of 15 of the class loaned to the SR for three months in 1953 whilst the 'Merchant Navy' Pacifics were out of action following the axle fracture suffered by No. 35020 at Crewkerne. No. 61329 was based at Stewarts Lane depot during its SR sojourn. *Transport Treasury – Eric Sawford*

Above No. 61329 is seen bowling along near Seamer with a Saturdays only (SO) service from Scarborough in August 1964. *Railphotoprints*

Below The other ER class to be found at Cohen's yard was the 'O4'. Originally introduced in 1911 to a Great Central design there were a number of variants, the five examples at Cransley all being of the 'O4/8' variant dating from 1944 having been rebuilt with 100A ('B1') boilers but retaining the original cylinders. No. 63644 is seen here (left) in March 1966. *Keith Partlow*

Two more examples, Nos. 63674 and 63675, both withdrawn in January 1966 from Colwick depot (16B), are seen on 17 April 1966. *Transport Treasury – Eric Sawford*

Above No. 63816 stands next to a classmate, both seemingly pretty complete although heavily work-stained in this 1966 view.

Below No. 63873 was withdrawn in January 1966, promptly sold to Cohen's in March and is seen in their yard in May. The final quartet of the 'O4/8' class to remain in BR service was withdrawn in April 1966. No. 63601 has been preserved and now forms part of the National Collection. *Both Keith Partlow*

11

BR Steam Locomotives Scrapped at Cransley – Standards

Class 4 4-6-0 No. 75041 was withdrawn in January 1968 and placed in store at Carnforth depot until sold to Cohen's later that year. Both this locomotive and the adjacent Stanier 'Black 5' No. 44889 have been separated from their tenders in this 9 May 1968 view. *Transport Treasury – Eric Sawford*

Above With a foreground of recovered boiler tubes Standard Class 4 2-6-0 No. 76042, late of Oxley shed, is seen on 11 December 1966. Note the plentiful supply of 16T mineral wagons stacked up behind the locomotive. *Derek Fear*

Below Standard Class 4 2-6-0 No. 76095 was one of five of the class handled by the yard. This example completed just less than 10 years' service before withdrawal from Chester shed came in September 1967.

Above A couple of ex SR Standard tanks Nos. 82013 and 82025 are seen on Kettering shed, adjacent to the turntable pit, on 22 November 1964 before a transfer trip onto the Loddington branch would take them to Cohen's yard. Six of these Class 3 2-6-2Ts were purchased from Nine Elms depot in London at the end of 1964. *Transport Treasury – Eric Sawford*

Below A token exchange is made between the signalman of Tipton St. Johns box and the crew of a smartly turned out No. 82013 as it passes with a Sidmouth service in August 1959. *Railphotoprints – Dave Cobbe*

Above Locomotives large and small were dealt with at Cohen's and none came more massive than the Standard Class 9F 2-10-0s of which eight examples were dealt with at Cransley. No. 92013 managed just over 12 years in traffic, much of the time on the Great Central, a paltry figure although not as bad as some of its classmates which barely managed five years before their premature withdrawal. It was withdrawn from Saltley shed in October 1966, arriving at the scrapyard in January 1967 and is seen here in March before being cut in May. *John Evans*

Below Little remains to indicate that this was once one of the most powerful freight locomotives built for BR. Reduced to piles of scrap No. 92090 was photographed on 2 February 1968. *David Hills*

No. 92181, based for most of its life at New England shed, ended up at Cohen's where it is seen on 30 May 1965 before final despatch in July. *Transport Treasury – Eric Sawford*

12

BR Diesel Locomotives Scrapped at Cransley – Shunters

A couple of the former WR 350hp diesel electric shunters Nos. 15101 and 15105 are seen in the yard in these views taken on 11 December 1969. They were based on the standard LMS shunter and constructed at Swindon Works in 1948 and withdrawn in August 1967. Behind 15101 is an 0-6-0ST Stewarts & Lloyds No. 39 from Storefield. *Both John Evans*

Above Cohen's made a practice of commandeering the odd locomotive to act as their yard shunter and following withdrawal by BR in May 1968 ex-Plymouth Laira Class 03 shunter No. D2176 fulfilled this role. Seen on 21 June 1970 it did not survive for much longer and was cut up during November 1971. The 'door to door' Conflat containers stacked up to the rear of the shunter were once a common sight on British Railways. When first introduced their livery was BR carriage crimson with straw lettering but this gave way towards the end of the 1950s to BR bauxite with white lettering, the words 'BRITISH RAILWAYS' being replaced with the arrow and the words 'door to door'. *Gordon Edgar*

Below An example of one of the 'door to door' containers mounted on a Conflat wagon in use at Hertford east goods yard in 1965. The wagon is BR 13T CONFLAT 'A' No. B705895; the container is BD6623B.

Parked alongside Cohen's rail-mounted yard crane is Class O4 shunter D2241 which had been delivered to New England depot in 1956 and which was withdrawn by BR in May 1971. It was used at Cransley as the yard shunter for a time and scrapped here in 1976. *Peter Robins*

Opposite above Class 10 shunter D4093 in a partially demolished state is seen in March 1969 with a couple more shunters plus No. 814, a 4wDM Ruston & Hornsby unit Class 48DS dating from 1943 which ended its operational days at the MOD Bicester Military Railway and was subsequently sold on by Cohen's to Morriston Depot at Swansea. *Grahame Wareham*

Opposite below Former London Midland Region Engineering Department 0-4-0 shunter ED3, built by Fowler and dating from 1943, is seen in January 1968. It was one of seven Fowler shunters of the class in use by the Engineers' Department. *Grahame Wareham*

13
BR Diesel Locomotives Scrapped at Cransley – Mainline

Above A couple of Beyer Peacock 'Hymeks' meet their Waterloo at Cransley on 8 March 1975 with D7001 nearest the camera. D7001 entered traffic in July 1961 and lasted until May 1974. A Class 501 EMU car No. M61140 is seen on the left. *Peter Robins*

Below Two years before D7001 leaves Cranmore with empty bitumen tanks bound for Westbury on 20 July 1973. *Railphotoprints –Gordon Edgar*

Above What might be termed an 'exploded view' of a Hymek believed to be D7026. Five examples of these diesel hydraulic locomotives were scrapped at Cransley. *Peter Robins*

Below One of the less than successful 'Baby Deltics' had reached the end of the line when D5906 was captured on film on 11 December 1969. Barely 10 years old this was a dramatic illustration of the shortcomings of the BR diesel pilot scheme which saw many dreadful designs limp on until put out of their misery prematurely at great cost to the taxpayer. Note the pile of scrap cars which had apparently added to the scope of the scrapyard's activities by this date. *John Evans*

Above Withdrawn in September 1968, D8202 is seen in August 1969 adjacent to other members of its short-lived class. *Grahame Wareham*

Below British-Thompson-Houston (BTH) supplied 10 Type 1 locomotives for local freight and e.c.s. duties originally in East Anglia in 1957. An order for a further 34 locomotives followed with delivery being between 1959 and 1961. Local Authorities in the London area were keen to implement the Clean Air Act seeing the removal of steam locomotives as a way of improving the quality of the air so the locomotives were transferred to East London. Under the TOPS numbering system the fleet was classified as Class 15 although none of the locomotives ever carried a new number. With the decline of London freight duties in the late 1960s the fleet of 44 locomotives found themselves redundant and withdrawals took place between 1969 and 1971, with the last members of the class being withdrawn from traffic on 27 March 1971. D8227 is seen here in August 1969 at Cohen's who went on to scrap 13 of the class at Cransley. *Graham Wareham*

Above D8213 was another of this 'baker's dozen' to reach this scrapyard and is seen awaiting its fate in August 1969. One member of the class, D8233, survives and is currently on the East Lancashire Railway. *Grahame Wareham*

Below A sunny day for a change at Cransley with a trio of these Type 1 Bo-Bo locomotives headed by D8236. *G. W. Sharpe courtesy Grahame Wareham*

A couple of April 1969 views of North British Type 1s, latterly Class 16. D8403 above heads a trio comprising D8402 and D8400. D8400 is marshalled next to an ex LMS coach with oval lavatory window in blue/grey livery. These locomotives were to spend the bulk of their short working lives at Stratford depot in East London. *Both George Woods*

Left D8403 is seen in this head-on view indicating the relatively good external condition in which these locomotives were withdrawn. D8403 was one of this small class of 10 built by the North British Co. in 1958 and being non-standard and rather unreliable they were obvious candidates for early withdrawal. They were all taken out of service between February and September 1968 and had been cut up for scrap by the end of 1969. *George Woods*

Below D8402 seen in August 1969. *Graham Wareham*

Bottom Framed by rosebay willowherb, which loves to colonise scrapyards and waste ground, D8401 waits to be dealt with by the scrapmen. *Graham Wareham*

Two further examples of Class 16 are D8405 and D8407, the latter being seen marshalled next to a DMU coach. *Both Graham Wareham*

D8400 and D8407 are seen at Stratford depot in April 1967 during their brief working lives of just 10 years. Inadequate ventilation resulted in frequent engine seizures and coolant contamination of the oil due to cylinder head failures was another recurrent problem with this design. They were fitted with a non-standard type of electro-magnetic control equipment (coded 'red circle' by BR) which was prone to failure and more importantly meant they could not operate in multiple with locomotives fitted with the more common electro-pneumatic ('blue star') controls. Unsurprisingly none were preserved. *Both Railphotoprints – Mike Jefferies*

14

Spotlight on the 'Baby Deltics'

This 10-strong class of diesel electric locomotives was built by the English Electric Company in 1959 at Vulcan Foundry as part of BR's pilot diesel scheme which was designed to review the performance of a number of varying designs of specific power ranges. The power unit used was a Napier Deltic T9-29 pressure charged 9-cylinder engine of 1,100bhp (820kW) at 1,600rpm driving a generator which powered the four traction motors and were mounted on two axle bogies given a Bo Bo configuration. They were numbered from D5900 to D5909 and latterly under TOPS became Class 23. With the exception of the engine the major mechanical parts were entirely standard save for the addition of trip-cock apparatus for use when being used on the Metropolitan 'Widened Lines' to Moorgate. Deliveries commenced in Spring 1959 to Hornsey Depot, via Doncaster Works for acceptance trials, the locos

20 October 1968	D5907 condemned.
30 December 1968	D5900 and D5903 condemned.
20 January 1969	D5904 condemned.
9 March 1969	D5908 condemned.
June 1969	D5900, D5903 and D5904 cut up at Cohen's, Cransley.
July 1969	D5906 and D5907 cut up at Cohen's, Cransley.
6 September 1969	D5901 taken to BR Research at Derby for use as motive power for the Tribometer train.
23 November 1969	D5902 condemned.
December 1969	D5908 cut up at Cashmore's, Great Bridge.
August 1970	D5902 cut up at Cohen's, Cransley.
14 February 1971	D5905 condemned.
12 March 1971	D5905 hauled to Stratford DRS, power unit 388 removed and kept as a spare for D5901.
7 March 1971	D5909 condemned.
August 1973	D5905 and D5909 cut up at Cohen's, Cransley.
December 1969	D5901 withdrawn.
18 February 1976	D5901 hauled to BR Doncaster Works.
March 1977	D5901 became the final 'Baby Deltic' to be cut up.

Seen at King's Cross wearing the attractive two-tone green livery D5907 awaits its next turn of duty in April 1967.
Railphotoprints – Mike Jefferies

transferring to the new Finsbury Park diesel depot upon its completion in 1960. At weekends they were often to be found at Hitchin Depot. It had been BR's original intention to work the locos on cross London freights on the Widened Lines but the locomotives were found to be too heavy in spite of the fitting of lightweight Oleo buffers and a reduction in the planned water carrying capacity. On initial completion the first locomotives were found to exceed the specified weight thus a programme of lightening was begun which involved cutting circular holes into the bogie frames and replacing steel buffer beams and roof panels with aluminium. Much of this excess weight was due to ancillary components such as the train-heating steam generators being supplied over weight. To avoid waste these components were replaced by lighter versions from other makers but the originals were then used in the Class 20 and Class 40 locomotives where excess weight was not an issue. The lightened locomotives eventually met with BR's approval but only after a painstaking weighing procedure that even involved specifying the exact amount of sand that could be carried in the sandboxes. They were allocated to King's Cross inner and outer suburban duties such as the Cambridge Buffet Express and sometimes on services from Kings Cross to Moorgate sub-surface platforms via the Widened Lines although they were later banned from Moorgate because of excessive exhaust smoke in the tunnels. Problems in service meant that by November of their first year seven engines had been required to be changed. The consequent reduction in availability meant that they were compared

unfavourably with the more reliable Class 24 Type 2. The Type 2s were averaging 30-40,000 miles per failure; the 'Baby Deltics' less than a quarter of this. By October 1960 no less than 44 engine changes had been made across the 10 examples. Four main engine problems were apparent:

• Fractured cylinder liners from the injector hole caused by assembly stresses.
• Fractured cylinder liners from the injector hole caused by electrolytic corrosion.
• Turbocharger bearing failures caused by exhaust gases leaking through the labyrinth seals.
• Seized pistons due to poor cooling caused by chemical erosion from incorrect lubricants.

In July 1961 BR suggested replacing the Napier engine with an English Electric 8SVT V8 but this would have added eight tons in extra weight and thus was rejected. As originally delivered they certainly could not be considered a successful design and as they failed they were all stored at Stratford Depot by June 1963. It was decided by BR and English Electric to undertake a refurbishment programme modifying the engines with new parts designed by the engine manufacturer. This was completed by 15 April 1965 and was a considerable improvement on the original and their aesthetic appearance was also tidied up, losing their gangway doors and headcode discs with centre headcode boxes. The BR diesel green was changed to the more attractive two-tone green livery similar to that carried by their larger sisters of Type 5, later TOPS Class

D5904 is not entrusted with a prestige Pullman duty but is merely making a smoky exit from King's Cross with the empty stock of the Yorkshire Pullman on 3 December 1967. *Railphotoprints*

55, to whom they bore a strong resemblance, hence their soubriquet 'Baby Deltic'. Only one of the class, D5909, carried the standard BR blue livery but a couple of others did sport the modern BR motif whilst continuing to carry green livery. Returning to traffic their performance was much improved although coolant problems persisted. Being such a small class of locomotives their non-standard status finally got the better of them and in 1968 they began to fall victim to the BR Standardisation Plan, the first of the class, D5906, being taken out of service in May and being condemned in October. The remainder of the class followed fairly quickly.

Thus all the locomotives were reduced to scrap, Cohen's at Cransley taking no less than eight of them. The only major component of a 'Baby Deltic' to survive is Napier T9-29 engine No. 388 along with its main and auxiliary

generators. It was stored at Stratford TMD as a spare for D5901 whilst it continued in service at Derby. After D5901 was finally withdrawn the decision was taken to transfer the engine to the NRM at York. In 2001 the engine was purchased by the Baby Deltic Project and restored to operational condition in 2008. The Project team also purchased Class 37 37372 into which the engine was temporarily fitted whilst undergoing running tests. In September 2010 the Baby Deltic Project announced its plans to recreate a replica of the class. This is being achieved through shortening 37372's body in three places and mounting it on Class 20 bogies. The locomotive can be viewed in the Barrow Hill Roundhouse near Chesterfield where it is currently undergoing the transformation from 37372 into what will hopefully become D5910.

Above By May 1973, the date of this upper view taken at Stratford, time was up for the 'Baby Deltics' and D5909, in company with D5905, awaits the call to the scrapyard of George Cohen.

Below Several members of the class were to be held at Stratford awaiting sale to scrap merchants including this pair of which D5905 is the leading locomotive. D5905 had been hauled to Stratford in March 1971 only to have its power unit removed as a spare for D5901 which was not scrapped until 1976. The power unit was purchased by the group hoping to build a new Class 23 using parts from a Class 37 and a Class 20. *Both Railphotoprints*

Above 'Baby Deltic' D5902, condemned in November 1969, is dumped at 30A Stratford TMD on 7 June 1970. This Class 23 was sandwiched between Class 11 Darlington-built 350hp shunters 12128 and 12106 also withdrawn from service. *Gordon Edgar*

Below One of the eight members of this small class of ten locomotives dealt with in August 1969 at Cransley is No. D5903. *Grahame Wareham*

Above A view of D5906, the first of the class to be condemned in May 1968, is seen in Cohen's yard during August 1969 sandwiched between coaching stock including BR maroon-livered Mark 1 Open Second No. E3869 dating from 1953. *Grahame Wareham*

Below The project to resurrect a Class 23 is taking shape inside Barrow Hill roundhouse in March 2011. Briefly the project aims to shorten the nose and body length of a Class 37, restyle the body and mount the locomotive on Class 20 bogies so as to reproduce, as far as is reasonably practicable, the appearance of a Class 23. *Ashley Dace licensed under Wikipedia Creative Commons Attribution Share-alike license*

15
BR Diesel Multiple Units
Scrapped at Cransley

BR blue 'Derby Lightweight' driving trailer M79184 awaiting the torch on 21 June 1970. It was built in July/August 1956 and was lent to Llandudno Junction initially prior to allocation to Manchester for that area's diesel scheme. These power twin set units, classified Driving Motor Brake Second (DMBS), were originally ordered for the hilly Buxton route, being allocated to Longsight depot. *Gordon Edgar*

Above Still in its original green livery, 'Derby Lightweight' motor coach E79025 is awaiting its fate on 21 June 1970. This DMBS, built in 1955, was initially destined for the Lincolnshire diesel scheme but in 1959 was transferred to East Anglia. They had a non standard 'yellow diamond' coupling code and were all to be withdrawn between September 1967 and July 1968. *Gordon Edgar*

Below A green-liveried Derby Lightweight unit is captured in service in the Home Counties operating a St Albans to Watford service in early 1965.

16
BR Electric Locomotives Scrapped at Cransley

The sole example of this class to reach Cransley was 74006, formerly E5023, which was rebuilt as electro-diesel No. E6106 in March 1968, becoming 74006 under the TOPS scheme. It was withdrawn in June 1976, over a year before the other conversions, due to fire damage. It is seen here in July 1977. *David Hills*

17
BR Coaching and Freight Stock Scrapped at Cransley

A considerable amount of coaching and freight stock was handled by Cohen's. Some of the more interesting items were a number of horseboxes from the SR, previously stored at Micheldever north of Winchester, which were transferred to Cransley in late 1971. These had been built in 1954 at the Earlestown Carriage Works and the following are known to have been dealt with – 96361, 96373, 96374, 96375, 96384, 96388, 96491, 96402, 96412. No. 96403 has been preserved at the Buckinghamshire Railway Centre and although a number did survive the majority were converted to other purposes such as generator cars. The only survivors believed to be still in original condition are the one mentioned above and a further example based at the NRM (National Railway Museum).

The majority of the coaches dealt with were withdrawn as life expired or surplus to operating requirements, having been replaced with newer designs or by other units such as DMUs. In a few cases accident or fire damage led to withdrawal and such was the case with coach No. 1624, a 1960 Kitchen/Buffet car built by Cravens. It was noted in March 1973 at Cricklewood with severe fire damage and

was later moved to Wolverton Coach Works. However, a year later in August 1974 it was noted at Kettering station sidings and two weeks later was taken into Cohen's yard at Cransley where it was despatched shortly afterwards.

Coach No. 25900 was derailed in May 1972 at Chathill near Eltham and was severely damaged losing one whole side of its bodywork. The remainder of the bodywork was burnt on site whilst the underframe was moved initially to Bricklayers Arms, thence to Brent and then to Chaddesden near Derby in October 1972. It finally arrived at Cohen's in January 1973 and was scrapped shortly after arrival.

One of the few escapees from the yard was W13085, bought from Cohen's for use as a dog training centre at Melton Mowbray for sniffing out drugs. It was later broken up on site due to concerns re asbestos contamination. A couple of coaches were sold on to preservation societies, the Keighley & Worth Valley Railway (KWVR) and the Great Central Railway, but these were also later scrapped. There was the occasional movement in the reverse direction when a coach which was originally preserved on the KWVR in 1973 was received by Cohen's for scrapping in March 1975.

In use for sniffer dog training is Cohen's escapee coach No. W13085. *Dave Evans*

Above Amongst the eclectic mix of coaching stock which Cohen's handled was this Cafeteria car M256M seen on 14 February 1965. *Transport Treasury – Eric Sawford*

Below Another venerable vehicle was M45039M seen in a pretty parlous external condition on 30 May 1965. *Transport Treasury – Eric Sawford*

Two further examples of some of the coaching stock broken up at Cransley are M9472M and M20760M seen below. Both images date from 1965. *Both Transport Treasury – Eric Sawford*

Two ancient 13T wooden-bodied wagons, both marked 'One journey only – Loco coal', were to be found in the yard on 14 March 1965. Note traces of the former owner's name and the location 'Nottingham' showing through the faded livery on the bottom example. *Both Transport Treasury – Eric Sawford*

Above Brake vans a-plenty were also to be seen at Cransley, this example being from the SR and numbered S56071. The painted cross in a circle was the tell-tale sign of condemned status. It was photographed on 21 May 1967. *Transport Treasury – Eric Sawford*

Below This 20T brakevan had obviously been condemned on 13 May 1965, according to the painted endorsement on the side, and had arrived at the yard very soon after being captured 17 days later on 30 May 1965. *Transport Treasury – Eric Sawford*

London Transport stock scrapped at Cransley

Above Adding much needed colour to the sombre shades of the scrapyard were a number of LT Underground cars which were captured at Cransley on 4 April 1964. They were dwarfed by the S15 No. 30507 seen alongside in the lower view. The first conveyance of pre 1938 LT stock had left Ruislip on 1 June 1960 bound for Cohen's site at Kingsbury (Tamworth). Stock went initially from Neasden to Bird's Long Marston, King's of Newmarket and Booth's of Rotherham; a small number of cars also went from here to Cohen's and Cashmore's. At Bird's in 1978, for example, there were over 40 cars of LT stock present. Several cars of vintage stock are preserved at the LT Museum in Covent Garden. Two-car CO stock dating from 1937/39 was seen at Cohen's Kettering as late as 29 December 1979. Cohen's here did not take pre 1938 stock until 1964 when their Hereford site at Rotherwas Junction had ceased operation. Some cars of 1931/4 MCCW DMS stock were also noted at Kettering in April 1964.

Left Car number 3327 has been preserved at the LT Museum in Covent Garden and represents a generation of tube trains known as 'Standard stock' which were constructed between 1923 and 1934. All Standard stock cars had air-powered doors, instead of attendant-controlled gates at the ends, which greatly increased the speed passengers could board at stations. The traction control equipment was housed behind the driver's cab and took up a lot of room. Standard stock formed the principal trains on the Piccadilly and Central lines until the early 1960s when they were replaced by 1959/62 stock. *Both Ron Fisher*

Two views of vintage LT Underground stock in service at Drayton Park depot on 11 April 1964. On 4 October 1975 the line was closed and ceased to be part of London Underground, being transferred to BR. On 8 August 1976 Drayton Park reopened as part of the national network with trains running to Old Street and on 8 November the same year the line was opened for services from Moorgate to Finsbury Park and beyond. Following the transfer of the line to British Rail the tube train car sheds at Drayton Park became redundant.

The track in the former four-road Underground sheds and outside in the yard seen in the above view had only been used by slow-moving empty tube trains so was in very good condition. It was subsequently purchased for re-use by the Festiniog Railway. *Both Ron Fisher*

Above A reminder of what the interior of vintage Underground stock looked like is provided by this view taken on 11 April 1964. *Ron Fisher*

Below Taken on 25 May 1979 an unidentified Class 31 shunting at Cransley passes a rake of redundant LT tube stock waiting to be taken into the scrapyard. This may well be some of the Aylesbury two-car CO/CP stock mentioned previously. The view was taken from the A43 road bridge looking towards the junction with the main line at Kettering. *Lewis Bevan*

19
Industrial Diesel and Steam Locomotives Scrapped at Cransley

This standard gauge four-wheel petrol-mechanical shunter, No. 600 Nellie, seen here in the scrapyard on 21 June 1970, started life as an armour-plated ex-First World War narrow gauge Motor Rail 'Simplex'. It was converted to a standard gauge petrol shunter by Kent Construction Ltd (Works No. 1553 of 1927) who later sold it on as a 'new loco' to Kettering Urban District Council for use at their Northfield Plant Depot. It was chain driven with the engine being mounted centrally between the frames. It passed to Cohen's on 8 October 1963 and had been scrapped by them by the end of December 1973. *Gordon Edgar*

Above Around 1984 a trio of Ruston & Hornsby four-wheel diesel mechanical '48DS' class locos await their fate, having been acquired from Railcar Services Ltd (formerly Wagon Repairs Ltd) at Wellingborough which closed in December 1983. In the line-up are works No. 224345 of 1945 (formerly-MOD Longmoor Military Railway), works No. 393303 of 1956 and works No. 235517 of 1945. *Gordon Edgar collection*

Below The scrapyard shunter assisting ex-BR Class 03 No. D2176, seen on page 77, on 21 June 1970, was this John Fowler 0-4-0 diesel mechanical. Works No. 4210143, built in 1958, originally worked for the Ministry of Power at Rawcliffe near Goole and at Chorley as their No.6 locomotive and later at Portishead power station. It was subsequently disposed of by Cohen's to Chettles Feather Hair Products of Wymington near Bedford as a stationary generator, without wheels or cab, in early 1975. It soon moved on to E. M. Cox Ltd. of Peterborough in a similar capacity where it was finally scrapped about 1987. The worksplate from this locomotive realised £50 when auctioned in April 2015. *Gordon Edgar*

Left On 21 September 1965 this unidentified former Oxfordshire Ironstone mines Peckett 0-4-0ST was caught on film passing through Northampton en route to Cohen's at Cransley. *John Evans*

Below A couple of unidentified Andrew Barclay 0-4-0STs are seen adjacent to the A43 road bridge over the Loddington branch in December 1966. The remains of an 0-6-0ST which has already lost its cab and tanks lies behind. *Both Derek Fear*

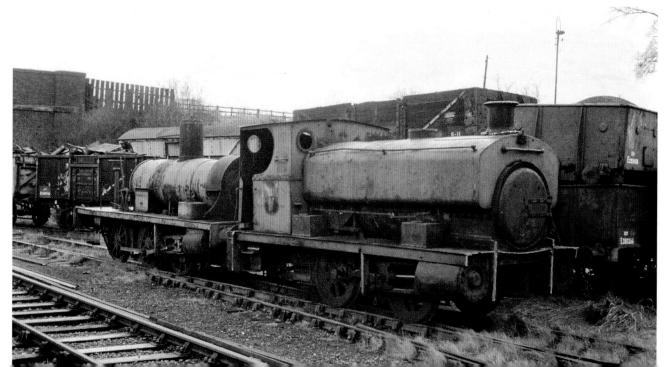

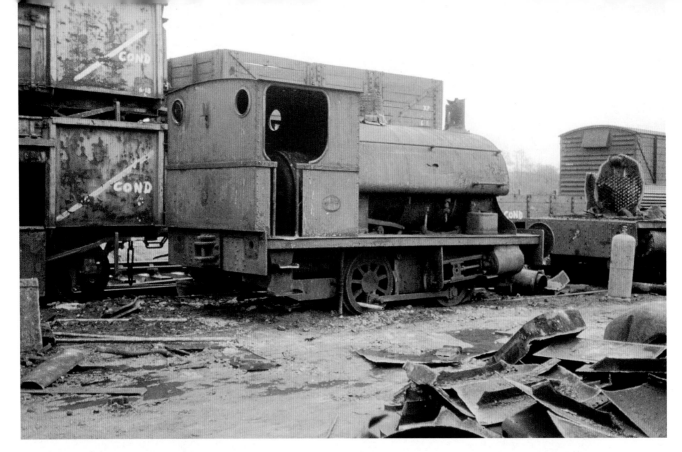

Above A Peckett 0-4-0ST sits amongst the debris adjacent to some stacked steel and wooden-bodied wagons. These ex Oxfordshire Ironstone Co. locomotives carried names, the rusty mark on the saddle tank side indicating their former position. *Derek Fear*

Below This Hunslet 0-6-0ST from Glendon Quarries is No 80 *Geddington* (HE2417/1941) which ran as Glendon Quarries No 3 prior to renumbering to 80 as part of the S&L Minerals fleet. Although the photographer was informed that the locomotive had been reserved for preservation, as witnessed by the covering over the chimney and sheeting over the cab, sadly this did not happen and it went on to be scrapped. It is seen positioned next to what was Cohen's yard shunter at the time. *John Evans*

Above S&L Minerals No. 39, Kitson 5477/1936 ex Corby, Glendon and Storefield Quarries, is seen in company with a couple of diesel shunters. This was one of the last steam locomotives to inhabit the yard here and may well have been the final steam locomotive to have been scrapped by Cohen's at this location. The date is 11 December 1969. *John Evans*

Below 0-4-0ST *Norseman* was built in 1921 by Andrew Barclay (Works No. 1711) and worked formerly at Tunnel Cement at Pitsford as its liberal coating of cement dust might indicate. The scale of this industrial locomotive is more in keeping with that of the adjacent LT Underground stock. Notice the huge dumb buffers.

20
Northamptonshire Ironstone Remembered

The following images capture the last days of the once thriving ironstone industry in Northamptonshire.
   Quarry workers warm themselves around a brazier as Andrew Barclay 0-4-0 saddle tank '19' (works No. 2101 of 1940) arrives with empty iron ore tipplers at the quarry loading point at Storefield Ironstone Quarry, Newton, near Kettering in the 1960s. *Gordon Edgar collection*

Right Former Kettering Iron & Coal Ltd 3ft gauge Manning Wardle 0-6-0 saddle tank 'Kettering Furnaces No. 8' (works No. 1675 built in 1906) is seen in the ironstone pits near Kettering on 23 May 1961. The workings here ceased in December 1962.

Below Bagnall 0-6-0 saddle tank 'Loddington No. 2' (works No. 2655 of 1942) in the quarry at Staveley Minerals Ltd. Cranford in the mid-1960s. *Both Gordon Edgar collection*

This page and opposite top Two views of Andrew Barclay 0-6-0 saddle tank 'Stainby' (works No. 2313 of 1951) with loaded iron ore tipplers at Stewarts & Lloyds Ltd, Buckminster Quarry, in June 1966. *Gordon Edgar collection*

Below 3ft 3in gauge Peckett 0-6-0 saddle tank (works No. 2029 of 1942) with a train at an unprotected crossing on the Wellingborough Ironstone Quarries system of Stewarts & Lloyds Minerals Ltd in the summer of 1966. *Gordon Edgar collection*

Appendices – Scrapping database

BR STEAM LOCOMOTIVES BELIEVED TO HAVE BEEN SCRAPPED BY COHEN'S AT THEIR KETTERING SITE

CLASS	LOCOMOTIVES	TOTALS
WESTERN REGION		
5700 0-6-0PT	3605, 3607, 3622, 3625	4
2800 2-8-0	3852	1
5700 0-6-0PT	4649	1
4073 4-6-0	5018 *St Mawes Castle*	1
5600 0-6-2T	6656, 6679, 6692	3
6800 4-6-0	6808 *Beenham Grange*, 6831 *Bearley Grange*, 6833 *Calcot Grange*, 6839 *Hewell Grange*, 6853 *Morehampton Grange*, 6855 *Saighton Grange*, 6861 *Crynant Grange*, 6871 *Bourton Grange*, 6879 *Overton Grange*	9
4900 4-6-0	6928 *Underley Hall*	1
7200 2-8-2T	7218	1
7400 0-6-0PT	7431	1
5700 0-6-0PT	8718, 8767, 9640	3
(WR total = 25)		
SOUTHERN REGION		
S15 4-6-0	30497, 30507, 30509, 30514	4
H16 4-6-2T	30518	1
Q 0-6-0	30549	1
V 4-4-0	30902 *Wellington*, 30921 *Shrewsbury*, 30935 *Sevenoaks*	3
W 2-6-4T	31912, 31914, 31922, 31924	4
Q1 0-6-0	33002, 33008, 33013, 33016, 33024	5
(SR total = 18)		
MIDLAND REGION		
2 2-6-2T	41212, 41219, 41228, 41326, 41327	5
1F 0-6-0T	41712	1
4 2-6-4T	42083, 42086, 42133, 42224, 42233, 42267	6
4 2-6-0	43004, 43018, 43051, 43098, 43129, 43130	6
4F 0-6-0	43928, 43951, 43988	3
4F 0-6-0	44109, 44113, 44171, 44182, 44191, 44244, 44260, 44278, 44284, 44380,	

5 4-6-0	44441, 44470, 44492, 44529, 44540, 44572, 44575, 44577, 44581	**19**
	44659, 44661, 44678, 44680, 44681, 44695, 44696, 44708, 44715, 44768, 44773, 44777, 44802, 44812, 44814, 44815, 44816, 44821, 44834, 44838, 44842, 44848, 44851, 44853, 44860, 44870, 44877, 44878, 44889, 44897, 44899, 44903, 44906, 44929, 44930, 44944, 44947, 44965, 45003, 45005, 45019, 45024, 45038, 45040, 45046, 45050, 45057, 45069, 45070, 45071, 45095, 45104, 45109, 45134, 45147, 45191, 45240, 45242, 45253, 45256, 45276, 45278, 45290, 45298, 45302, 45303, 45308, 45312, 45343, 45353, 45375, 45376, 45412	**73**
2 2-6-0	46495, 46519	**2**
3F 0-6-0T	47318, 47355, 47384, 47396, 47397, 47410, 47435, 47437, 47447, 47482, 47494, 47500, 47501, 47521, 47530, 47535, 47615, 47649, 47658, 47661, 47674	**21**
8F 2-8-0	48036, 48064, 48088, 48162, 48202, 48225, 48256, 48270, 48272, 48282, 48304, 48327, 48338, 48372, 48374, 48394, 48424, 48467, 48514, 48527, 48536, 48542, 48617, 48631, 48632, 48683, 48739, 48755	**28**

(MR total = 164)

EASTERN REGION

B1 4-6-0	61042, 61121, 61145, 61158, 61250 *A Harold Bibby*, 61329, 61360, 61406	**8**
04 2-8-0	63644, 63674, 63675, 63816, 63873	**5**

(ER total = 13)

STANDARD CLASSES

4 4-6-0	75041	**1**
4 2-6-0	76008, 76036, 76041, 76042, 76095	**5**
3 2-6-2T	82011, 82012, 82013, 82014, 82025	**5**
9F 2-10-0	92013, 92036, 92090, 92100, 92103, 92142, 92143, 92181	**8**

(Standard total = 19)

Although Standard 4-6-0s 75040/42 were listed as scrapped at Cransley by Peter Hands in his books What happened to steam' these have been shown to be fabrications by the What Really Happened To Steam (WHRTS) team who are currently working to compile an accurate record of disposals. Recent further amendments have seen the addition of 76036 and 82025 and the removal of 76015 from the Cransley database.

TOTAL   **239**

BR DIESEL LOCOMOTIVES BELIEVED TO HAVE BEEN SCRAPPED BY COHEN'S AT THEIR KETTERING SITE

CLASS	LOCOMOTIVES	TOTAL
03 0-6-0 DM SHUNTER	(originally numbered D2000–D2199, D2370–D2399, later renumbered 03004–03399) D2015, D2100, D2131, D2176, D2372, D2374, D2375, D2376, D2380, D2384, D2390, D2391, D2395, D2396, 03004, 03007, 03009, 03035, 03044, 03068, 03076, 03095, 03102, 03105, 03110, 03163, 03171, 03172, 03386	**29**
04 0-6-0 DM SHUNTER	(originally 11100–60, which became D2200-41, 11212-29 which became D2242-59, and D2260-D2341) 11102, D2220, D2223, D2236, D2241, D2253	**6**
10 0-6-0 DE SHUNTER	(originally 13137–13166, which became D3137–D3151, D3439–D3453, D3473–D3502, D3612–D3651, D4049–D4094) D3143, D3440, D3441, D3444, D3477, D3479, D3483, D3485, D3488, D3491, D3492, D3494, D3612, D3615, D3629, D3633, D3635, D3637, D3640, D3643, D4049, D4054, D4058, D4059, D4063, D4066, D4071, D4073, D4075, D4078, D4079, D4086, D4087, D4090, D4093, D4094	**36**
11 0-6-0 DE SHUNTER	(numbered 12033–12138) 12038, 12056, 12067, 12068, 12072, 12075, 12076, 12078, 12087, 12096, 12101, 12102, 12113, 12116, 12124, 12134, 12138	**17**

14 0-6-0 DH SHUNTER	(numbered D9500–9555) D9509, D9519	**2**
15 BTH TYPE 1 BO-BO	(numbered D8200–8243) D8202, D8205, D8208, D8212, D8213, D8217, D8219, D8223, D8227, D8235, D8236, D8238, D8240	**13**
16 NB TYPE 1	(numbered D8400–8409) D8400, D8401, D8402, D8403, D8405, D8407, D8408, D8409	**8**
23 EE 'BABY DELTIC' BO-BO	(numbered D5900-5909) D5900, D5902, D5903, D5904, D5905, D5906, D5907, D5909	**8**
24 SULZER TYPE 2 BO-BO	(numbered D5000–5150, renumbered 24001–24047/24051–24141) D5088	**1**
35 BEYER PEACOCK HYMEK B-B	(numbered D7000–D7100) D7001, D7022, D7026, D7028, D7093	**5**
D3/11 0-6-0 DE SHUNTER	(numbered 15101–15106) 15101, 15105, 15106	**3**
D3/3	0-6-0 DE SHUNTER (numbered 13117–13126, renumbered D3117–3126) D3120, D3125	**2**
ENGINEERING DEPT.	ED3	**1**

TOTAL 131

BR ELECTRIC LOCOMOTIVES BELIEVED TO HAVE BEEN SCRAPPED BY COHEN'S AT THEIR KETTERING SITE

CLASS	LOCOMOTIVES	TOTAL
70 SR CO-CO	(numbered 20001-3) 20003	1
74 ELECTRO-DIESEL CO-CO	(numbered E6101–6110, renumbered 74001–10, rebuilds of E5XXX electric locomotives) 74006 (rebuilt from E5023)	1
TOTAL	**2**	

INDUSTRIAL STEAM LOCOMOTIVES BELIEVED TO HAVE BEEN SCRAPPED BY COHEN'S AT THEIR KETTERING SITE

New Cransley No. 3 0-4-0ST	1194/1900 Chapman & Furneaux, rebuilt 1952 Holywell iron Works	ex Cransley Iron & Steel Co.
0-4-0ST	832/1900 Peckett	ex Cransley Iron & Steel Co.
Norseman 0-4-0ST	1711/1921 Andrew Barclay	ex Tunnel Cement Pitsford
Alex 0-6-0ST	3716/1952 Hunslet	ex Oxfordshire Ironstone Wroxton
Grace 0-4-0ST	1894/1936 Peckett	ex Oxfordshire Ironstone Wroxton
Maud 0-4-0ST	1937/1938 Peckett	ex Oxfordshire Ironstone Wroxton
John (*Joan* until 8/1957) 0-6-0ST	1981/1940 Peckett	ex Oxfordshire Ironstone Wroxton
Mary 0-4-0ST	1818/1950 Hudswell Clarke	ex Oxfordshire Ironstone Wroxton
Barabel 0-4-0ST	1868/1953 Hudswell Clarke	ex Oxfordshire Ironstone Wroxton
Betty 0-4-0ST	1869/1953 Hudswell Clarke	ex Oxfordshire Ironstone Wroxton
Joan 0-4-0ST	1822/1919 Avonside	ex Oxfordshire Ironstone Wroxton
Jean (*Betty* until 5/1958) 0-4-0ST	1696/1939 Hudswell Clarke	ex Oxfordshire Ironstone Wroxton
Phyllis 4wVBT	9615/1956 Sentinel	ex Oxfordshire Ironstone Wroxton
Progress 0-6-0ST	1402/1915 Peckett	ex South Durham Iron & Steel Irchester
Major 0-4-0ST	1363/1914 Andrew Barclay	ex South Durham Iron & Steel Irchester
Rothwell 0-4-0ST	1258/1912 Peckett	ex South Durham Iron & Steel Irchester
No. 16 0-4-0ST	3892/1936 Hawthorn Leslie	ex South Durham Iron & Steel Irchester
No. 8 0-4-0ST	1609/1918 Andrew Barclay	ex South Durham Iron & Steel Irchester
No. 6 0-6-0ST	1497/1916 Andrew Barclay	ex British Steel Corp Irchester
Holwell No. 30 0-4-0ST	3780/1932 Hawthorn Leslie	ex British Steel Corp Irchester
No. 7 0-4-0ST	2324/1952 Andrew Barclay	ex British Steel Corp Irchester
No. 2 50 Carmarthen 0-6-0ST	5478/1936 Kitson	ex British Steel Corp Irchester
No. 17 0-4-0ST	3946/1937 Hawthorn Leslie	ex British Steel Corp Irchester
No. 20 0-4-0ST	2143/1942 Andrew Barclay	ex British Steel Storefield
No. 19 0-4-0ST	2101/1940 Andrew Barclay	ex British Steel Storefield

Enterprise 0-4-0ST	1739/1907 Bagnall	ex British Steel Storefield
No. 39 49 *Caerphilly* 0-6-0ST	5477/1936 Kitson	ex British Steel Storefield
No. 80 No.3 0-6-0ST	2417/1941 Hunslet	ex British Steel Corp Glendon East
Pilton 0-6-0ST	1832/1919 Avonside	ex British Steel Corp Pilton
52 0-6-0ST	7004/1940 Robert Stephenson & Hawthorns	ex British Steel Corp Gretton Brook Corby
0-4-0F	1492/1916 Andrew Barclay	ex Laporte Chemicals Luton & Peterborough Heavy Haulage Yaxley

TOTAL 31

SCRAPPED BY COHEN'S AT LODDINGTON

New Cransley No. 3 0-6-0ST	3883/1936 Hawthorn Leslie	ex Appleby- Frodingham Steel Co.
No. 7 0-6-0ST	3884/1936 Hawthorn Leslie	ex Appleby- Frodingham Steel Co.
William Ellis 0-6-0ST	2054/1930 Avonside	Metre gauge supplied new to Loddington quarries; originally intended for Singapore Harbour

TOTAL   **3**

COHEN'S ALSO VISITED OTHER SITES LOCALLY TO SCRAP LOCOMOTIVES IN SITU ONE EXAMPLE BEING THE BRITISH STEEL CORPORATION CORBY QUARRIES WHERE THE FOLLOWING WERE DESPATCHED

Criggion 0-6-0ST	5476/1936 Kitson	ex Stewarts & Lloyds Corby
46 *Cardigan* 0-6-0ST	5473/1933 Kitson	ex Stewarts & Lloyds Corby
53 0-6-0ST	7030/1941 Robert Stephenson & Hawthorns	ex Stewarts & Lloyds Corby
58 0-6-0ST	7668/1950 Robert Stephenson & Hawthorns	new
59 0-6-0ST	7670/1950 Robert Stephenson & Hawthorns	new
61 0-6-0ST	7672/1950 Robert Stephenson & Hawthorns	new
64 0-6-0ST	8050/1950 Robert Stephenson & Hawthorns	new

TOTAL   **7**

INDUSTRIAL DIESEL LOCOMOTIVES BELIEVED TO HAVE BEEN SCRAPPED BY COHEN'S AT THEIR KETTERING SITE

ED3 0-4-0DM	4200042/1949 John Fowler & Co. Leeds	ex BR Bedford
PM22 0-4-0DM	6967/1939 Robert Stephenson & Hawthorns	ex CAEC Howard Ltd. Bedford
PM23 0-4-0DM	6968/1939 Robert Stephenson & Hawthorns	ex CAEC Howard Ltd. Bedford
DS1169 4wDM	237923/1946 Ruston & Hornsby	ex BR Yeovil Junction
247 0-4-0DM	342/1940 Andrew Barclay	ex MOD Bicester
No. 11 0-4-0DM	4679/1955 Hunslet	ex NCB Tilmanstone Colliery, Kent
0-6-0DH	6691/1968 Hunslet	ex NCB Woolley Colliery, South Yorks.

TOTAL   **7**

INDUSTRIAL DIESEL LOCOMOTIVES BELIEVED TO HAVE BEEN USED BY COHEN'S ON SITE AT CRANSLEY OR SOLD ON

Kett 22 *Nellie* 4wPM	1553/1927 Kent Construction & Eng. Co.	ex Kettering Borough Council scrapped by 1973
D2241 0-6-0DM	D291/1956 Vulcan Foundry/Drewry	ex BR Colchester Depot scrapped 1976
D2176 0-6-0DM	1961 Swindon Works	ex BR Crewe Works scrapped by 1971

TOTAL 3

Kett 39 4wDM	386871/1955 Ruston & Hornsby	ex cargo Fleet scrapyard to Kingsbury Depot Warwick
2 0-4-0DM	19024/1930 John Fowler & Co.	ex Canning Town depot to Barking Works Essex
814 4wDM	218046/1943 Ruston & Hornsby	ex MOD Bicester to Morriston Depot Swansea
0-4-0DM	4210143/1958 John Fowler & Co.	ex Ministry of Power, Portishead to Chettles Feather Hair Products, Wymington
4wDM	252841/1948 Ruston & Hornsby	ex E Midlands Gas Board, Northampton to Kingsbury Works
2484C 0-4-0DM	4200022/1948 John Fowler & Co.	ex Vauxhall Motors Luton to Weldit Eng., Barrow
26443C 0-4-0DM	4210012/1950 John Fowler & Co.	ex Vauxhall Motors Luton disposal unknown
850 0-4-0DM	2068/1940 Hunslet	ex MOD Bicester to Chettles Feather Hair Products, Wymington
4wDH	27544/1959 North British (Queens Park Works)	ex West Midlands Gas Board, Birmingham to Chettles Feather Hair Products. Wymington
0-4-0DM	23010/1945 John Fowler	ex MOD Hartlebury to Motherwell Machinery & Scrap
221 0-4-0DM	22968/1942 John Fowler	ex MOD Hartlebury to Pollock Brown & Co., Northam
268 0-4-0DM	23009/1944 John Fowler	ex MOD Hartlebury to Salford Depot Lancs.
03 018 600 No. 2 0-6-0DM	1958 Swindon	ex BR Depot Norwich to Pollock Brown & Co., Northam
243 0-4-0DM	22890/1939 John Fowler	ex MOD Bicester to 600 Ferrous Fragmentizers Ltd., Willesden
9038 2w – 2PMR	8198/1958 Wickham & Co. Ware	ex MOD Bicester to Dart Valley Railway
4wDM	9922/1959 Motor Rail, Simplex Works Bedford	ex London Brick Co. Calvert disposal unknown

TOTAL   **16**

Key

DM	Diesel – mechanical transmission
PM	Petrol/paraffin - mechanical transmission
DH	Diesel – hydraulic transmission
R	Railcar - passenger vehicle
4w	Four wheel – no connecting rods
F	Fireless

DIESEL MULTIPLE UNITS BELIEVED TO HAVE BEEN SCRAPPED BY COHEN'S AT THEIR KETTERING SITE

CLASS	UNITS
Cravens Class 112 DMCL	51712, 51714, 51725
BR Derby Class 108 DMBS	51915
Cravens Class 129 DMPMV	55998
BR Derby Class 108 DTCL	56211
Gloucester RCW Class 100 DTCL	56310
BR Derby DMBS	79025, 79028, 79044
Metro-Cammell DMBS	79048, 79049, 79050, 79051, 79052, 79054, 79065, 79068
BR Derby DMBS	79119, 79121, 79123, 79127, 79129, 79145
BR Derby DMBS	79180, 79184
BR Derby DTCL	79259, 79260, 79261
Metro-Cammell DTSL	79263, 79264, 79265, 79267, 79275, 79278, 79279, 79281, 79284
BR Derby DTCL	79610, 79615, 79633/79191*, 79635/79193*, 79640, 79657, 79668, 79672, 79673, 79678

The majority of DMUs were scrapped in 1970/1 although the earliest was in June 1967 and the latest in July 1980. One unit, 55988, spent five years in the yard 1975 –80, whilst another, 56310, survived for almost 6 years 10/74– 7/80 before despatch. *Renumbered

TOTAL   **48**

ELECTRIC MULTIPLE UNITS BELIEVED TO HAVE BEEN SCRAPPED BY COHEN'S AT THEIR KETTERING SITE

Class 501	M61140
4 SUB	S11302S (part of Set 4621)

TOTAL   **2**

BR MK 1 COACHING STOCK BELIEVED TO HAVE BEEN SCRAPPED BY COHEN'S AT THEIR KETTERING SITE

TYPE	BUILT	NUMBERS
Restaurant/Buffet Converted from restaurant First	1970/71	1624
Restaurant Unclassified built	1957 (Ashford/Swindon)	1905, 1906
Open First	1954 (BRCW)	3004, 3006
Tourist Open Second	1951/2 (York 1951) (Cravens 1952)	3702, 3713, 3720
Open Second	1954 (Derby)	3722, 3724, 3725
Open Second	1953 (Doncaster/York)	3739, 3742, 3756, 3768, 3773, 3774, 3782, 3783, 3786, 3788, 3793, 3806, 3808, 3822, 3841, 3862, 3867, 3869, 3882
Open Second	1954/5 (Ashford/Eastleigh) (York)	3891, 3956, 3972, 3997
Open Second	1956/7 (Ashford/Swindon)	4036
Open Second	1955/6 (York) (BRCW)	4111, 4136, 4141, 4143, 4146, 4168, 4175, 4183, 4188, 4283 (4238?), 4326, (4397?)
Open Second	1956/7 (York)	4505, 4601, 4612
Open Second	1957/8 (York)	4670, 4765
Open Brake Second	1955/6 (Doncaster)	9238, 9240
Corridor First	1951 (Swindon)	13026, 13047
Corridor First	1953 (Swindon)	13068, 13076, 13081, 13085++
Corridor First	1954 (Swindon)	13095, 13112, 13119, 13123

Corridor First	1955 (Swindon)	13143, 13144, 13155, 13161, 13165, 13168, 13180, 13181, 13183
Corridor First	1957–9 (Ashford/Swindon)	13192, 13207, 13208, 13210, 13216, 13217
Corridor Composite	1952 (Eastleigh) (Derby)	15000, 15001, 15012
Corridor Composite	1951/2 (Ashford/Eastleigh)	15022, 15032, 15049
Corridor Composite	1953 (Metro Cammell)	15077, 15079, 15091, 15096*, 15097, 15109, 15111, 15145, 15183, 15203, 15211, 15226, 15234, 15245
Corridor Composite	1952/3 (Cravens)	15275, 15285, 15289
Corridor Composite	1953 (Derby)	15343, 15366, 15367, 15377, 15381, 15386, 15395, 15405, 15418, 15419, 15428
Corridor Composite	1953/4 (Metro Cammell)	15460, 15466, 15472, 15479, 15486, 15494, 15506, 15508, 15519, 15521, 15534, 15537
Corridor Composite	1955 (Metro Cammell)	15573, 15576
Corridor Composite	1954/55 (BRCW)	15586, 15604, 15611+, 15618, 15621
Corridor Composite	1956 (Wolverton)	15641
Corridor Composite	1955/6 (Metro Cammell)	15717, 15775, 15781, 15792, 15808, 15826, 15828, 15875, 15877, 15915
Corridor Composite	1956/7 (Wolverton)	15940
Corridor Composite	1963 (Derby)	16260
Corridor Brake Composite	1954/5 (Metro Cammell)	21037, 21050, 21073, 21074
Corridor Brake Composite	1956 (Metro Cammell)	21119, 21120
Corridor Brake Composite	1955/6 (Charles Roberts)	21168
Corridor Brake Composite	1958/9 (Charles Roberts)	21169, 21172, 21178, 21180
Corridor Second	1951 (Derby)	24001, 24002, 24028, 24040, 24053, 24072, 24073, 24076, 24080, 24137, 24159, 24162, 24172
Corridor Second	1951/2 (Doncaster)	24210, 24214
Corridor Second	1951/2 (York)	24240, 24267, 24282
Corridor Second	1952 (Ashford/Eastleigh)	24305, 24311, 24313, 24321
Corridor Second	1953 (BRCW)	24332, 24337, 24339, 24340, 24348, 24382, 24387
Corridor Second	1953 (Derby)	24401, 24402, 24403
Corridor Second	1954 (Swindon)	24468, 24492, 24494, 24508, 24517, 24530, 24537
Corridor Second	1952 (York)	24539
Corridor Second	1954 (York)	24554, 24569, 24571
Corridor Second	1953 (BRCW)	24587, 24612, 24616, 24641, 24651, 24653, 24661
Corridor Second	1953 (Cravens)	24694, 24712, 24715
Corridor Second	1954 (Swindon)	24746, 24749, 24758, 24759, 24773, 24780
Corridor Second	1954 (BRCW)	24801
Corridor Second	1955/6 (Derby)	24823, 24863, 24920, 24930, 24937, 24946, 24970, 24978
Corridor Second	1955/6 (Wolverton)	25048, 25095, 25101, 25120, 25133, 25138, 25147, 25158
Corridor Second	1957 (Metro Cammell)	25188, 25206, 25234, 25246
Corridor Second	1957/8 (Metro Cammell)	25272
Corridor Second	1957 (Doncaster)	25457
Corridor Second	1957/8 (Wolverton)	25628
Corridor Second	1961/2 (Derby)	25708, 25900
Corridor Brake Second	1951/2 (Derby)	34065, 34088
Corridor Brake Second	1951/2 (Wolverton)	34106, 34119, 34176
Corridor Brake Second	1952 (Ashford/Eastleigh)	34230, 34233, 34243, 34250
Corridor Brake Second	1952 (Wolverton)	34285
Corridor Brake Second	1953/4 (Wolverton)	34308, 34321, 34322, 34323, 34326, 34328, 34337, 34347
Corridor Brake Second	1952/3 (Wolverton)	34381, 34416, 34433
Corridor Brake Second	1953 (GRCW)	34492, 34493

Corridor Brake Second	1954 (Charles Roberts)	34519
Corridor Brake Second	1955 (Wolverton)	34564, 34570
Corridor Brake Second	1955 (GRCW)	34592
Corridor Brake Second	1954/5 (Charles Roberts)	34652
Corridor Brake Second	1955 (Wolverton)	34686, 34711, 34717, 34776
Corridor Brake Second	1956 (GRCW)	34816, 34817, 34823, 34826, 34829
Corridor Brake Second	1956/7 (Metro Cammell)	34955
Composite with lavatory (Non gangwayed)	1954/5 (Doncaster)	43002, 43009, 43026, 43030, 43039, 43048
Composite with lavatory (Non gangwayed)	1954/5 (York)	43112, 43113, 43127, 43160
Composite with lavatory (Non gangwayed)	1954/5 (Swindon)	43175, 43226
Composite with lavatory (Non gangwayed)	1955 (York)	43290, 43294, 43295
Second (Non gangwayed)	1953/4/5 (Swindon)	46005, 46036#, 46089
Second (Non gangwayed)	1954 (Wolverton)	46111
Second (Non gangwayed)	1954/5 (Derby)	46208, 46216, 46225, 46238, 46306
Second open with lavatory (Non gangwayed)	1955 (Doncaster)	48002, 48010~, 48030
Departmental vehicle		975026

Sold on to Gloucestershire & Warwickshire Railway but scrapped in 11/99
#Underframe converted to carflat
~Acquired from KWVR
+broken up on GCR 3/99
++Sold for drug sniffer dog training

BIBLIOGRAPHY

The Ironstone Quarries of the Midlands Part 5 The Kettering Area, Eric Tonks
The End of the Line, Eric Sawford
The Cransley & Loddington Branch (*Railway Bylines* August and September 2014), Barry Taylor
Railway Magazine February 1991 and October 1995, Eric Sawford
British Rail Coaching Stock Mk. 1 Coaches, Ashley Butlin
Diesel and Electric Locomotives for Scrap, Ashley Butlin
Diesels and Electrics for Scrap Vol. 1, Ashley Butlin
Steam for Scrap Vols. 1-3, Nigel Trevena
From Steam to the Scrapyard, Alan Earnshaw
Steam for Sale, Alan Earnshaw
Last Rites from the Track to the Scrapyard, John Evans
Industrial Locomotives of Buckinghamshire, Bedfordshire & Northamptonshire, Robin Waywell
RCTS *Railway Observer* magazine

PHOTOGRAPHIC CONTRIBUTORS

Lewis Bevan
John Chalcraft (Rail Photoprints)
Tom Curtis
Gordon Edgar
Dave Evans
John Evans
Derek Fear
Ron Fisher
David Hills
Derek Jones
Bob Martin

Keith Partlow
Geoff Plumb
RCTS photographic archive
Peter Robins
The Transport Treasury (Eric Sawford, Stephen Summerson and Leslie Freeman collections)
Grahame Wareham
George Woods
Peter Yarlett

Index of Images

Other books from Crecy by Jeffery Grayer featuring locomotive scrapyards

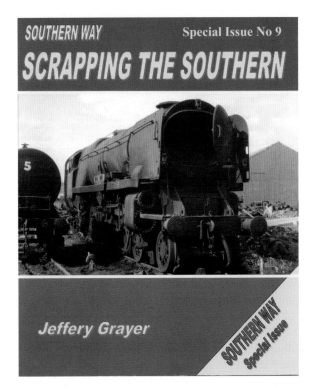

Southern Way Special Issue No 9 Scrapping the Southern

Paperback, 120 pages
ISBN: 9781909328044
£16.50

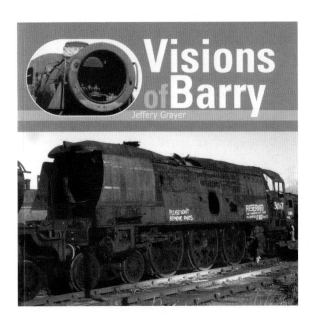

Visions of Barry

Paperback, 128 pages
ISBN: 9781909328495
£14.95

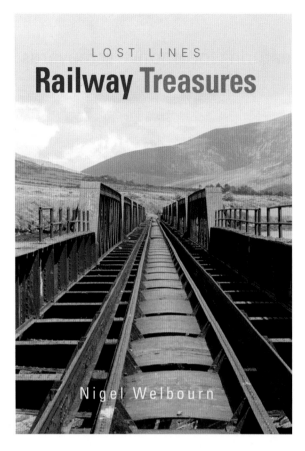

Lost Lines: Railway Treasures

Nigel Welbourn

Many readers will be familiar with Nigel Welbourn's long-running and best-selling *Lost Lines* series in 15 volumes, each covering a different part of the country.

In this new book, Welbourn takes an overview of what has been lost from a national perspective. The book spans the temporary closure of the Oystermouth Railway in the 1820s to the Folkestone Harbour branch closure in 2014.

Railway Treasures takes us on a journey through a huge variety of closed lines, including those abandoned by the 'Big Four' post-1923, as well as those lost in the savage cuts of the Beeching era. It offers an intriguing perspective on what remains of many lines and stations, from the largest structures to tiny relics of past glories.

Most of the book's 400 colour photographs have never been published before. Over 200 stations and halts, 75 tunnels and viaducts, and 40 docks, ports, quays and harbours are included, as well as a treasure trove of maps, tickets and other items of railway ephemera. This book will delight not only railway enthusiasts but will appeal to a much wider cadre of readers with an interest in the British countryside and our transport and industrial heritage.

Hardback, 256 pages
ISBN: 9780860936916
£25.00

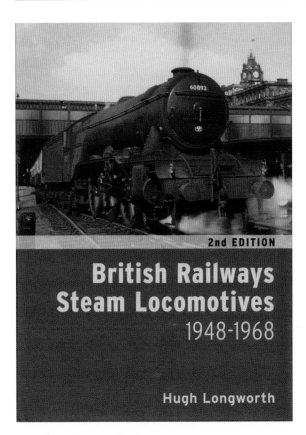

British Railways Steam Locomotives
1948-1968

Hugh Longworth

First published in 2005, Hugh Longworth's monumental work chronicling each steam locomotive operated by British Railways between 1 January 1948 and the end of main line steam in August 1968 has become a standard work of reference. Since the book's first publication, the author has been updating and correcting the information enabling the publication of a completely revised second edition. This edition includes data and illustrations of many of the classes and as a new feature, line drawings of each locomotive class listed in the book.

Covering all the locomotives inherited in 1948 as well as those constructed post-Nationalisation, the book identifies precisely the history of each individual locomotive. Information provided includes technical data, modifications, date of construction, names, date of withdrawal and much more, thus providing the reader with a single-volume reference to the many thousands of steam locomotives operated between 1948 and the end of main line steam.

Hardback, 360 pages
ISBN: 9780860936602
£45.00

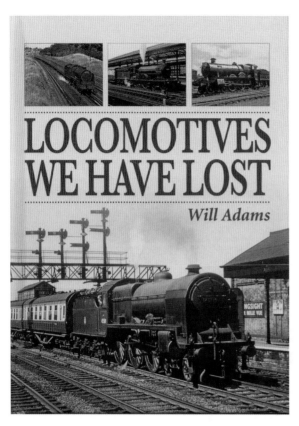

Locomotives We Have Lost

Will Adams

Locomotives We Have Lost is a large and comprehensive compilation of information and reference photographs of the steam locomotives that did not survive into preservation, effectively becoming extinct.

This book contains an introductory account of the phased withdrawal of the steam locomotives under BR in the 1950s and 1960s and also includes a short description of each class accompanied by a reference photograph of a locomotive in that class. Each picture presented has the detail of the story behind that particular locomotive.

There is a useful appendix which gives a complete listing of all the classes under BR ownership, showing which became extinct and which lived on in preservation.

Locomotives We Have Lost serves as a fitting tribute to the steam locomotive classes that have been lost to our railway heritage and is an essential book for all railway enthusiasts.

Hardback, 260 pages
ISBN: 9780860936671
£35.00

Atlas of Rail Station Closures

A valuable new work of railway reference, the *Atlas of Railway Station Closures* maps all the standard gauge railway lines built in Britain and lists the dates when each line and every station on those lines was closed. The company, BR Region or later organisation owning the station at the time of the closure is listed, as well as the last pre-grouping owner. The name of the station used is, in every instance, that applied at the time of its closure

Encompassing a wealth of invaluable information organised and presented in an easily accessible format, the *Atlas of Railway Station Closures* includes comprehensive cartographic mapping of the entire railway network of Britain showing its railway station closures, a complete easy to use index and gazetteer listing the date of each closure and a photographic section illustrating some of these lost stations.

An invaluable and comprehensive record and a fascinating insight into the history and development of Britain's railway network, the *Atlas of Railway Station Closures* is a must have reference for the bookshelves of any railway enthusiast, local historian and anyone with an interest in Britain's industrial heritage.

Hardback, 153 pages
ISBN: 9780860936770
£25.00

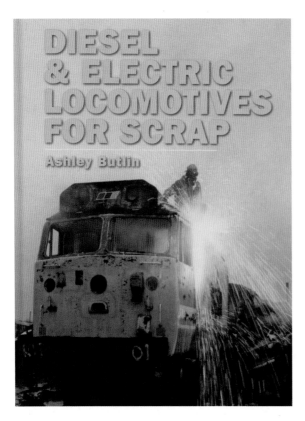

Diesel and Electric Locomotives for Scrap

Ashley Butlin

Diesel and Electric Locomotives for Scrap is adetailed survey of all diesel and electric locomotives scrapped on Britain›s railways since the start of British Railways in 1948 to the present day. While it does not include DMUs and EMUs, the book lists each locomotive class separately, and within each class lists each locomotive built with details of every locomotive scrapped.

Comprehensively illustrated throughout in black and white and colour, this book shows examples of each class, recorded when scrapped and also contains a separate section showing all preserved heritage diesel and electric locomotives on Britain›s railways today.

Author Ashley Butlin has compiled this wealth of information intending this book to be as near a complete record of all diesel and electric locomotives scrapped in this period as possible, and as such it will be the ultimate work of reference for enthusiasts of modern traction.

Hardcover, 240 pages
ISBN: 9780860936701
£35.00